HEALING FOR TODAY HOPE FOR TOMORROW

Compiled by
Gary Wilde

A
JANET
THOMA
BOOK

Thomas Nelson Publishers
Nashville

140084

Other Books in the New Perspective™ Series

Free from the Past
Bible Promises for Adult Children Alcoholics
Hope for the Hungry Heart
Bible Promises for Overeaters
Renewed Each Day
Bible Promises for Overcoming Chemical Dependency

Published in Nashville, Tennessee, by Thomas Nelson, Inc., and distributed in Canada by Lawson Falle, Ltd., Cambridge, Ontario.

Scripture quotations are from the NEW KING JAMES VERSION of the Bible. Copyright © 1979, 1980, 1982, Thomas Nelson, Inc., Publishers.

Library of Congress Cataloging-in-Publication Data

Healing for today, hope for tomorrow / compiled by
 Gary Wilde.
      p.   cm.—(New perspectives)
   ISBN 0-8407-3245-7 (pbk.)
   1. Codependents—Religious life. 2. Christian
life—1960–   . I. Wilde, Gary. II. Series.
BV4596.C57H43   1992
248.8′6—dc20   92–3100
                                      CIP

Printed in the United States of America
1 2 3 4 5 6 7 — 96 95 94 93 92

CONTENTS

Introduction

You have chosen to walk the road to recovery—the path to serenity. At times along the way you will face seemingly impossible challenges and some painful realities in order to receive the health and peace you are longing for. *Healing for Today, Hope for Tomorrow* gives you the encouragement and strength you need for your journey with Scripture promises from the New King James Version of the Bible.

Each chapter takes you through a different step of recovery. And the Scripture passages within each chapter are fertile ground for you to begin sowing new choices and reaping lifelong benefits. You will find freedom from compulsions and hope for balance in your relationships. You will see the necessity of accountability and gain the wisdom you need to maintain your new lifestyle.

You may want to read this book from beginning to end. Or you may choose to turn to the section that relates to where you are today and read and meditate on those passages. But however you choose to use this book, keep it nearby for you to turn to anytime of the day.

Discover new perspectives for your life as you read God's words in *Healing for Today, Hope for Tomorrow*.

For Those Driven by Compulsions

Society admires the successful ones, those who "have it together." How do you get there? Many have found the standard terribly high, the price incredibly steep: loss of inner contentment in exchange for outward status.

A mind filled with thoughts about the next promotion, a spotless house, a perfect appearance, or a straight-A semester is never really freed up to face the pain, loneliness, anger, and hurt that are also a part of every life. These items do not rate high on the list of star qualities, but they are real and must not be ignored. Otherwise busy-ness and achievement become substitutes for personal wholeness. Getting ahead takes precedence over "getting a heart."

What drives you? Food, sex, money, fitness, alcohol, success? What keeps you from fully embracing the joy of living in close contact with your true self and with your God? It's more than just being able to stop and smell the roses occasionally. The Scriptures call us to walk in the garden and nowhere else!

Fleeing the Compulsion-Centered Life

But know this, that in the last days perilous times will come: For men will be lovers of themselves, lovers of money, boasters, proud, blasphemers, disobedient to parents, unthankful, unholy, unloving, unforgiving, slanderers, without self-control, brutal, despisers of good, traitors, headstrong, haughty, lovers of pleasure rather than lovers of God.

—2 TIMOTHY 3:1–4

■ *Facing My Failures*

Have mercy on me, O LORD, for I am in
   trouble;
My eye wastes away with grief,
Yes, my soul and my body!
For my life is spent with grief,
And my years with sighing;
My strength fails because of my iniquity,
And my bones waste away.
I am a reproach among all my enemies,
But especially among my neighbors,
And am repulsive to my acquaintances;
Those who see me outside flee from me.

I am forgotten like a dead man, out of mind;
I am like a broken vessel.
For I hear the slander of many;
Fear is on every side.

—PSALM 31:9–13

O Lord, do not rebuke me in Your wrath,
Nor chasten me in Your hot displeasure!
For Your arrows pierce me deeply,
And Your hand presses me down.
There is no soundness in my flesh
Because of Your anger,
Nor is there any health in my bones
Because of my sin.
For my iniquities have gone over my head;
Like a heavy burden they are too heavy for
  me.
My wounds are foul and festering
Because of my foolishness.
I am troubled, I am bowed down greatly;
I go mourning all the day long.
For my loins are full of inflammation,
And there is no soundness in my flesh.
I am feeble and severely broken;
I groan because of the turmoil of my heart.

—PSALM 38:1–8

■ Admitting My Weariness and Weakness

In labors more abundant, in stripes above measure, in prisons more frequently, in deaths often.

From the Jews five times I received forty stripes minus one. Three times I was beaten with rods; once I was stoned; three times I was shipwrecked; a night and a day I have been in the deep; in journeys often, in perils of waters, in perils of robbers, in perils of my own countrymen, in perils of the Gentiles, in perils in the city, in perils in the wilderness, in perils in the sea, in perils among false brethren; in weariness and toil, in sleeplessness often, in hunger and thirst, in fastings often, in cold and nakedness—besides the other things, what comes upon me daily: my deep concern for all the churches. Who is weak, and I am not weak?

—2 CORINTHIANS 11:23b–29

■ *Giving Up on Willpower*

The law is holy, and the commandment holy and just and good. Has then what is good become death to me? Certainly not! But sin, that it might appear sin, was producing death in me through what is good, so that sin through the commandment might become exceedingly sinful. For we know that the law is spiritual, but I am carnal, sold under sin. For what I am doing, I do not understand. For what I will to do, that I do not practice; but what I hate, that I do. If, then, I do what I will not to do, I agree with the law that it is good. But now, it is no longer I who do it, but sin that dwells in me.

For I know that in me (that is, in my flesh) nothing good dwells; for to will is present with me, but how to perform what is good I do not find. For the good that I will to do, I do not do; but the evil I will not to do, that I practice. Now if I do what I will not to do, it is no longer I who do it, but sin that dwells in me. I find then a law, that evil is present with me, the one who wills to do good. For I delight in the law of God according to the inward man. But I see another law in my members, warring against the law of my mind, and bringing me into captivity to the law of sin which is in my members. O wretched man that I am! Who will deliver me from this body of death? I thank God—through Jesus Christ our Lord!

—ROMANS 7:12-25

■ Putting Past Compulsions Behind Me

Therefore put to death your members which are on the earth: fornication, uncleanness, passion, evil desire, and covetousness, which is idolatry. Because of these things the wrath of God is coming upon the sons of disobedience, in which you once walked when you lived in them.

—COLOSSIANS 3:5-7

Therefore gird up the loins of your mind, be sober, and rest your hope fully upon the grace that is to be brought to you at the revelation of Jesus Christ; as obedient children, not conforming yourselves to the former lusts, as in your ignorance;

but as He who called you is holy, you also be holy in all your conduct, because it is written, "Be holy, for I am holy."

—1 PETER 1:13–16

Favoring the God-Centered Life

For the grace of God that brings salvation has appeared to all men, teaching us that, denying ungodliness and worldly lusts, we should live soberly, righteously, and godly in the present age, looking for the blessed hope and glorious appearing of our great God and Savior Jesus Christ, who gave Himself for us, that He might redeem us from every lawless deed and purify for Himself His own special people, zealous for good works.

—TITUS 2:11–14

Remove from me the way of lying,
And grant me Your law graciously.
I have chosen the way of truth;
Your judgments I have laid before me.
I cling to Your testimonies;
O LORD, do not put me to shame!
I will run in the way of Your commandments,
For You shall enlarge my heart.
Teach me, O LORD, the way of Your statutes,
And I shall keep it to the end.
Give me understanding, and I shall keep Your
    law;

Indeed, I shall observe it with my whole
    heart.
Make me walk in the path of Your
    commandments,
For I delight in it.
Incline my heart to Your testimonies,
And not to covetousness.
Turn away my eyes from looking at worthless
    things,
And revive me in Your way.

—PSALM 119:29–37

■ Going to God for Help

To You I will cry, O LORD my Rock:
Do not be silent to me,
Lest, if You are silent to me,
I become like those who go down to the pit.

—PSALM 28:1

Hear, O LORD, and have mercy on me;
LORD, be my helper!

—PSALM 30:10

Seeing then that we have a great High Priest
who has passed through the heavens, Jesus the
Son of God, let us hold fast our confession. For we
do not have a High Priest who cannot sympathize
with our weaknesses, but was in all points
tempted as we are, yet without sin. Let us therefore come boldly to the throne of grace, that we

may obtain mercy and find grace to help in time of
need.

—HEBREWS 4:14–16

■ Seeking God's Sovereignty over Every Power in My Life

"To whom then will you liken Me,
Or to whom shall I be equal?" says the Holy
  One.
Lift up your eyes on high,
And see who has created these things,
Who brings out their host by number;
He calls them all by name,
By the greatness of His might
And the strength of His power;
Not one is missing.
Why do you say, O Jacob,
And speak, O Israel:
"My way is hidden from the LORD,
And my just claim is passed over by my
  God"?
Have you not known?
Have you not heard?
The everlasting God, the LORD,
The Creator of the ends of the earth,
Neither faints nor is weary.
There is no searching of His understanding.
He gives power to the weak,
And to those who have no might He increases
  strength.

Even the youths shall faint and be weary,
And the young men shall utterly fall,
But those who wait on the LORD
Shall renew their strength;
They shall mount up with wings like eagles,
They shall run and not be weary,
They shall walk and not faint.

—ISAIAH 40:25-31

■ *Letting God Protect Me*

Hear my cry, O God;
Attend to my prayer.
From the end of the earth I will cry to You,
When my heart is overwhelmed;
Lead me to the rock that is higher than I.
For You have been a shelter for me,
A strong tower from the enemy.
I will abide in Your tabernacle forever;
I will trust in the shelter of Your wings.

—PSALM 61:1-4

My soul, wait silently for God alone,
For my expectation is from Him.
He only is my rock and my salvation;
He is my defense;
I shall not be moved.
In God is my salvation and my glory;
The rock of my strength,
And my refuge, is in God.

—PSALM 62:5-7

He who dwells in the secret place of the Most
   High
Shall abide under the shadow of the Almighty.
I will say of the LORD, "He is my refuge and
   my fortress;
My God, in Him I will trust."
Surely He shall deliver you from the snare of
   the fowler
And from the perilous pestilence.
He shall cover you with His feathers,
And under His wings you shall take refuge;
His truth shall be your shield and buckler.

—PSALM 91:1–4

■ Accepting God's Provision for My Deepest Desires

And the Spirit and the bride say, "Come!" And
let him who hears say, "Come!" And let him who
thirsts come. And whoever desires, let him take
the water of life freely.

—REVELATION 22:17

Do not fret because of evildoers,
Nor be envious of the workers of iniquity.
For they shall soon be cut down like the grass,
And wither as the green herb.
Trust in the LORD, and do good;
Dwell in the land, and feed on His
   faithfulness.
Delight yourself also in the LORD,

And He shall give you the desires of your
  heart. . . .
A little that a righteous man has
Is better than the riches of many wicked. . . .
The LORD knows the days of the upright,
And their inheritance shall be forever.
They shall not be ashamed in the evil time,
And in the days of famine they shall be
  satisfied. . . .
The steps of a good man are ordered by the
  LORD,
And He delights in his way. . . .
He is ever merciful, and lends;
And his descendants are blessed.

—PSALM 37:1-4, 16, 18-19, 23, 26

■ Overcoming My Thorn in Flesh through Christ's Power

And lest I should be exalted above measure by
the abundance of the revelations, a thorn in the
flesh was given to me, a messenger of Satan to
buffet me, lest I be exalted above measure. Concerning this thing I pleaded with the Lord three
times that it might depart from me. And He said to
me, "My grace is sufficient for you, for My
strength is made perfect in weakness." Therefore
most gladly I will rather boast in my infirmities,
that the power of Christ may rest upon me.

Therefore I take pleasure in infirmities, in re-
proaches, in needs, in persecutions, in distresses,

for Christ's sake. For when I am weak, then I am strong.

—2 CORINTHIANS 12:7–10

■ *Resisting Compulsions in God's Strength*

Where do wars and fights come from among you? Do they not come from your desires for pleasure that war in your members? You lust and do not have. You murder and covet and cannot obtain. You fight and war. Yet you do not have because you do not ask. You ask and do not receive, because you ask amiss, that you may spend it on your pleasures.

Adulterers and adulteresses! Do you not know that friendship with the world is enmity with God? Whoever therefore wants to be a friend of the world makes himself an enemy of God. Or do you think that the Scripture says in vain, "The Spirit who dwells in us yearns jealously"? But He gives more grace. Therefore He says:

"God resists the proud,
But gives grace to the humble."

Therefore submit to God. Resist the devil and he will flee from you. Draw near to God and He will draw near to you. Cleanse your hands, you sinners; and purify your hearts, you double-minded. Lament and mourn and weep! Let your laughter be turned to mourning and your joy to gloom.

Humble yourselves in the sight of the Lord, and He will lift you up.

—JAMES 4:1-10

■ *Trusting Christ for True Peace*

On the same day, when evening had come, He said to them, "Let us cross over to the other side."

Now when they had left the multitude, they took Him along in the boat as He was. And other little boats were also with Him. And a great windstorm arose, and the waves beat into the boat, so that it was already filling. But He was in the stern, asleep on a pillow.

And they awoke Him and said to Him, "Teacher, do You not care that we are perishing?"

Then He arose and rebuked the wind, and said to the sea, "Peace, be still!" And the wind ceased and there was a great calm. But He said to them, "Why are you so fearful? How is it that you have no faith?"

—MARK 4:35-40

For He Himself is our peace.

—EPHESIANS 2:14

For Those Tormented by the Past

For a very young child, it was just a silly, offhanded remark: "Let go of me! Don't ever touch me again." But her parents took her seriously—literally! They never really lovingly touched her again. No hugs, no gentle caresses, no encouraging pats on the back. What happens when you grow up like that? No doubt there will be some adult feelings of being left out, some fear of abandonment, a sense of never getting enough attention focused on you.

Codependent adults use lots of emotional energy rehearsing past regrets: Why couldn't they have just shown some affection? Why weren't they there when I needed them? Why didn't they help me more? This can have positive results when rehearsed and released, when forgiveness ultimately flows from a therapeutic re-experiencing of that childhood deprivation. Yet many of us cling to past hurts, using them to fuel current bitterness, letting

them justify our life of continued inner turmoil.

Facing Pain from the Family of Origin

■ *Feeling Denied of Parent's Blessings*

Then it happened, as soon as Isaac had finished
blessing Jacob, and Jacob had scarcely gone out
from the presence of Isaac his father, that Esau his
brother came in from his hunting.

He also had made savory food, and brought it to
his father, and said to his father, "Let my father
arise and eat of his son's game, that your soul may
bless me." And his father Isaac said to him, "Who
are you?" And he said, "I am your son, your first-
born, Esau."

Then Isaac trembled exceedingly, and said,
"Who? Where is the one who hunted game and
brought it to me? I ate all of it before you came, and
I have blessed him—and indeed he shall be
blessed." When Esau heard the words of his
father, he cried with an exceedingly great and bitter cry, and said to his father, "Bless me—even me
also, O my father!" . . . And Esau said to his
father, "Have you only one blessing, my father?
Bless me—even me also, O my father!" And Esau
lifted up his voice and wept.

—GENESIS 27:30-34, 38

■ Feeling Completely Abandoned

My God, My God, why have You forsaken
   Me?
Why are You so far from helping Me,
And from the words of My groaning?
O My God, I cry in the daytime, but You do
   not hear;
And in the night season, and am not silent.
But You are holy,
Who inhabit the praises of Israel.
Our fathers trusted in You;
They trusted, and You delivered them.
They cried to You, and were delivered;
They trusted in You, and were not ashamed.
But I am a worm, and no man;
A reproach of men, and despised of the
   people.
All those who see Me laugh Me to scorn;
They shoot out the lip, they shake the head,
   saying,
"He trusted in the LORD, let Him rescue Him;
Let Him deliver Him, since He delights in
   Him!"
But You are He who took Me out of the
   womb;
You made Me trust when I was on My
   mother's breasts.
I was cast upon You from birth.
From My mother's womb
You have been My God.

Be not far from Me,
For trouble is near;
For there is none to help.
Many bulls have surrounded Me;
Strong bulls of Bashan have encircled Me.
They gape at Me with their mouths,
As a raging and roaring lion.
I am poured out like water,
And all My bones are out of joint;
My heart is like wax;
It has melted within Me.
My strength is dried up like a potsherd,
And My tongue clings to My jaws;
You have brought Me to the dust of death.
For dogs have surrounded Me;
The assembly of the wicked has enclosed Me.
They pierced My hands and My feet;
I can count all My bones.
They look and stare at Me.
They divide My garments among them,
And for My clothing they cast lots.
But You, O LORD, do not be far from Me;
O My Strength, hasten to help Me!
Deliver Me from the sword,
My precious life from the power of the dog.
Save Me from the lion's mouth
And from the horns of the wild oxen!

—PSALM 22:1–21

Forgiving Family Sins of the Past

"'I beg you, please forgive the trespass of your brothers and their sin; for they did evil to you.' Now, please, forgive the trespass of the servants of the God of your father." And Joseph wept when [his family members] spoke to him. Then his brothers also went and fell down before his face, and they said, "Behold, we are your servants." Joseph said to them, "Do not be afraid, for am I in the place of God? But as for you, you meant evil against me; but God meant it for good" . . . And he comforted them and spoke kindly to them.

—GENESIS 50:17–20

Then Peter came to Him and said, "Lord, how often shall my brother sin against me, and I forgive him? Up to seven times?" Jesus said to him, "I do not say to you, up to seven times, but up to seventy times seven. . . . 'Should you not also have had compassion on your fellow servant, just as I had pity on you?'"

—MATTHEW 18:21–22, 33

Finding Reparenting through God

But now, O LORD,
You are our Father;
We are the clay, and You our potter;
And all we are the work of Your hand.

—ISAIAH 64:8

A father of the fatherless, a defender of
    widows,
Is God in His holy habitation.

—PSALM 68:5

"In My Father's house are many mansions; if it
were not so, I would have told you. I go to prepare
a place for you. And if I go and prepare a place for
you, I will come again and receive you to Myself;
that where I am, there you may be also. And
where I go you know, and the way you know."

Thomas said to Him, "Lord, we do not know
where You are going, and how can we know the
way?"

Jesus said to him, "I am the way, the truth, and
the life. No one comes to the Father except through
Me. If you had known Me, you would have known
My Father also; and from now on you know Him
and have seen Him."

Philip said to Him, "Lord, show us the Father,
and it is sufficient for us."

Jesus said to him, "Have I been with you so
long, and yet you have not known Me, Philip? He
who has seen Me has seen the Father."

—JOHN 14:2–9

■ A Parent Who Hears and Answers

You have answered Me.
I will declare Your name to My brethren;
In the midst of the congregation I will praise
    You.

You who fear the LORD, praise Him!
All you descendants of Jacob, glorify Him,
And fear Him, all you offspring of Israel!
For He has not despised nor abhorred the
 affliction of the afflicted;
Nor has He hidden His face from Him;
But when He cried to Him, He heard.
My praise shall be of You in the great
 congregation;
I will pay My vows before those who fear
 Him.
The poor shall eat and be satisfied;
Those who seek Him will praise the LORD.
Let your heart live forever!
All the ends of the world
Shall remember and turn to the LORD,
And all the families of the nations
Shall worship before You.
For the kingdom is the LORD's,
And He rules over the nations.
All the prosperous of the earth
Shall eat and worship;
All those who go down to the dust
Shall bow before Him,
Even he who cannot keep himself alive.
A posterity shall serve Him.
It will be recounted of the Lord to the next
 generation,
They will come and declare His righteousness
 to a people who will be born,
That He has done this.

—PSALM 22:21–31

■ A Parent Who Is There for Us

"Fear not, for I have redeemed you;
I have called you by your name;
You are Mine.
When you pass through the waters, I will be
    with you;
And through the rivers, they shall not
    overflow you. When you walk through the
    fire, you shall not be burned,
Nor shall the flame scorch you.
For I am the LORD your God,
The Holy One of Israel, your Savior;
I gave Egypt for your ransom,
Ethiopia and Seba in your place.
Since you were precious in My sight,
You have been honored,
And I have loved you;
Therefore I will give men for you,
And people for your life.
Fear not, for I am with you."

—ISAIAH 43:1-5

■ An Accepting Parent

"But in every nation whoever fears Him and
works righteousness is accepted by Him."

—ACTS 10:35

Grace to you and peace from God our Father
and the Lord Jesus Christ. Blessed be the God and
Father of our Lord Jesus Christ, who has blessed

us with every spiritual blessing in the heavenly places in Christ, just as He chose us in Him before the foundation of the world, that we should be holy and without blame before Him in love, having predestined us to adoption as sons by Jesus Christ to Himself, according to the good pleasure of His will, to the praise of the glory of His grace, by which He has made us accepted in the Beloved.

—EPHESIANS 1:2–6

You also, as living stones, are being built up a spiritual house, a holy priesthood, to offer up spiritual sacrifices acceptable to God through Jesus Christ.

—1 PETER 2:5

■ A Comforting Parent

"I, even I, am He who comforts you.
Who are you that you should be afraid
Of a man who will die,
And of the son of a man who will be made like grass?"

—ISAIAH 51:12

As one whom his mother comforts,
So I will comfort you;
And you shall be comforted.

—ISAIAH 66:13

Blessed be the God and Father of our Lord Jesus Christ, the Father of mercies and God of all comfort, who comforts us in all our tribulation, that we may be able to comfort those who are in any trouble, with the comfort with which we ourselves are comforted by God.

—2 CORINTHIANS 1:3-4

■ *A Loving Parent*

We have known and believed the love that God has for us. God is love, and he who abides in love abides in God, and God in him. Love has been perfected among us in this: that we may have boldness in the day of judgment; because as He is, so are we in this world. There is no fear in love; but perfect love casts out fear, because fear involves torment. But he who fears has not been made perfect in love. We love Him because He first loved us.

—1 JOHN 4:16-19

■ *A Gracious Parent*

But God, who is rich in mercy, because of His great love with which He loved us, even when we were dead in trespasses, made us alive together with Christ (by grace you have been saved), and raised us up together, and made us sit together in the heavenly places in Christ Jesus, that in the ages to come He might show the exceeding riches of His grace in His kindness toward us in Christ Jesus. For by grace you have been saved through faith, and that not of yourselves; it is the gift of

God, not of works, lest anyone should boast.

—EPHESIANS 2:4–9

For we ourselves were also once foolish, disobedient, deceived, serving various lusts and pleasures, living in malice and envy, hateful and hating one another. But when the kindness and the love of God our Savior toward man appeared, not by works of righteousness which we have done, but according to His mercy He saved us, through the washing of regeneration and renewing of the Holy Spirit, whom He poured out on us abundantly through Jesus Christ our Savior, that having been justified by His grace we should become heirs according to the hope of eternal life.

—TITUS 3:3–7

■ *An Inheritance-Granting Parent*

For as many as are led by the Spirit of God, these are sons of God. For you did not receive the spirit of bondage again to fear, but you received the Spirit of adoption by whom we cry out, "Abba, Father." The Spirit Himself bears witness with our spirit that we are children of God, and if children, then heirs—heirs of God and joint heirs with Christ, if indeed we suffer with Him, that we may also be glorified together.

—ROMANS 8:14–17

Even so we, when we were children, were in bondage under the elements of the world. But when the fullness of the time had come, God sent forth His Son, born of a woman, born under the law, to redeem those who were under the law, that we might receive the adoption as sons. And because you are sons, God has sent forth the Spirit of His Son into your hearts, crying out, "Abba, Father!" Therefore you are no longer a slave but a son, and if a son, then an heir of God through Christ.

—GALATIANS 4:3-7

■ *A Training Parent*

"My son, do not despise the chastening of the
    LORD,
Nor be discouraged when you are rebuked by
    Him;
For whom the LORD loves He chastens,
And scourges every son whom He receives."

If you endure chastening, God deals with you as with sons; for what son is there whom a father does not chasten? But if you are without chastening, of which all have become partakers, then you are illegitimate and not sons. Furthermore, we have had human fathers who corrected us, and we paid them respect. Shall we not much more readily be in subjection to the Father of spirits and live? For they indeed for a few days chastened us as seemed best to them, but He for our profit, that we may be partakers of His holiness. Now no chastening seems to be joyful for the present, but grievous; nevertheless, afterward it yields the peaceable fruit of righteousness to those who have been trained by it.

—HEBREWS 12:5–11

■ *A Guiding Parent*

So God led the people around by way of the wilderness of the Red Sea. And the children of Israel went up in orderly ranks out of the land of Egypt. . . . And the LORD went before them by day in a pillar of cloud to lead the way, and by night in a pillar of fire to give them light, so as to go by day and night. He did not take away the pillar of cloud by day or the pillar of fire by night from before the people.

—EXODUS 13:18, 21–22

He will feed His flock like a shepherd;
He will gather the lambs with His arm,
And carry them in His bosom,
And gently lead those who are with young.

—ISAIAH 40:11

Focusing on the Future

But as it is written:

"Eye has not seen, nor ear heard,
Nor have entered into the heart of man

The things which God has prepared for those
who love Him."
—1 CORINTHIANS 2:9

For we know that if our earthly house, this tent,
is destroyed, we have a building from God, a
house not made with hands, eternal in the heavens. For in this we groan, earnestly desiring to be
clothed with our habitation which is from heaven,
if indeed, having been clothed, we shall not be
found naked. For we who are in this tent groan,
being burdened, not because we want to be un-
clothed, but further clothed, that mortality may be
swallowed up by life. Now He who has prepared
us for this very thing is God, who also has given
us the Spirit as a guarantee. Therefore we are
always confident, knowing that while we are at
home in the body we are absent from the Lord.
—2 CORINTHIANS 5:1-6

And I saw a new heaven and a new earth, for
the first heaven and the first earth had passed
away. Also there was no more sea. Then I, John,
saw the holy city, New Jerusalem, coming down
out of heaven from God, prepared as a bride
adorned for her husband. And I heard a loud voice
from heaven saying, "Behold, the tabernacle of
God is with men, and He will dwell with them,
and they shall be His people, and God Himself
will be with them and be their God. And God will
wipe away every tear from their eyes; there shall

be no more death, nor sorrow, nor crying, and there shall be no more pain, for the former things have passed away."

—REVELATION 21:1–4

CHAPTER 3

For Those Experiencing
Low Self-Esteem

"I love and accept every part of me, uncondi-
tionally." Easy for you to say? Or virtually
impossible?

Jill never heard words of affirmation in her
family of origin. Mostly her mother criticized
Jill's plump body and harped at her about losing weight. Her father wasn't really mean or
unkind, he just never seemed to notice that Jill
had feelings. He was busy.

Lacking a deep sense of value and dignity,
Jill, as an adult, struggles with mental tapes
that constantly put her assumed inadequacies
on parade. She senses that she's missing
something everyone else seems to have. She
knows she's distressingly approval-oriented,
but she can't stand the idea of someone find-
ing fault with her. Constantly defending herself from criticism, she strives to be perfect in
every way. It's a draining routine. When will
she be able to lay her burden down?

Must I Always Feel So Guilty?

Blessed is he whose transgression is forgiven,
Whose sin is covered. . . .
For this cause everyone who is godly shall
     pray to You
In a time when You may be found;
Surely in a flood of great waters
They shall not come near him.
You are my hiding place;
You shall preserve me from trouble;
You shall surround me with songs of
     deliverance.
I will instruct you and teach you in the way
     you should go;
I will guide you with My eye.

—PSALM 32:1, 6-8

How Long Can I Keep Pretending to Be Perfect?

Also He spoke this parable to some who trusted in themselves that they were righteous, and despised others: "Two men went up to the temple to pray, one a Pharisee and the other a tax collector. The Pharisee stood and prayed thus with himself, 'God, I thank You that I am not like other men— extortioners, unjust, adulterers, or even as this tax collector. I fast twice a week; I give tithes of all that I possess.'

"And the tax collector, standing afar off, would not so much as raise his eyes to heaven, but beat his breast, saying, 'God, be merciful to me a sinner!'

"I tell you, this man went down to his house justified rather than the other; for everyone who exalts himself will be abased, and he who humbles himself will be exalted."

—LUKE 18:9–14

Will I Ever Stop Feeling Ashamed of Myself?

My dishonor is continually before me,
And the shame of my face has covered me.
—PSALM 44:15

You know my reproach, my shame, and my
    dishonor;
My adversaries are all before You.
—PSALM 69:19

In You, O LORD, I put my trust;
Let me never be put to shame.
—PSALM 71:1

Do not fear, for you will not be ashamed;
Nor be disgraced, for you will not be put to
    shame;
For you will forget the shame of your youth.
—ISAIAH 54:4

Instead of your shame you shall have double
    honor,
And instead of confusion they shall rejoice in
    their portion.
Therefore in their land they shall possess
    double;
Everlasting joy shall be theirs.

—ISAIAH 61:7

You shall eat in plenty and be satisfied,
And praise the name of the LORD your God,
Who has dealt wondrously with you;
And My people shall never be put to shame.
Then you shall know that I am in the midst of
    Israel,
And that I am the LORD your God
And there is no other.
My people shall never be put to shame.

—JOEL 2:26–27

Looking unto Jesus, the author and finisher of
our faith, who for the joy that was set before Him
endured the cross, despising the shame, and has
sat down at the right hand of the throne of God.

—HEBREWS 12:2

Why Can't I Seem to Trust Anyone?

God is not a man, that He should lie,
Nor a son of man, that He should repent.
Has He said, and will He not do it?

Or has He spoken, and will He not make it
   good?

—NUMBERS 23:19

And the heavens will praise Your wonders, O
   LORD;
Your faithfulness also in the congregation of
   the saints.
For who in the heavens can be compared to
   the LORD?
Who among the sons of the mighty can be
   likened to the LORD?
God is greatly to be feared in the assembly of
   the saints,
And to be held in reverence by all those who
   are around Him.
O LORD God of hosts,
Who is mighty like You, O LORD?
Your faithfulness also surrounds You. . . .
My covenant I will not break,
Nor alter the word that has gone out of My
   lips.

—PSALM 89:5–8, 34

Trust in the LORD with all your heart,
And lean not on your own understanding;
In all your ways acknowledge Him,
And He shall direct your paths.

—PROVERBS 3:5–6

For what if some did not believe? Will their unbelief make the faithfulness of God without effect?

Certainly not! Indeed, let God be true but every
man a liar.

—ROMANS 3:3-4

"Surely blessing I will bless you, and multiply-
ing I will multiply you." And so, after he had pa-
tiently endured, he obtained the promise. For men
indeed swear by the greater, and an oath for con-
firmation is for them an end of all dispute.

Thus God, determining to show more abundantly to the heirs of promise the immutability of
His counsel, confirmed it by an oath, that by two
immutable things, in which it is impossible for
God to lie, we might have strong consolation, who
have fled for refuge to lay hold of the hope set before us. This hope we have as an anchor of the
soul, both sure and steadfast, and which enters
the Presence behind the veil.

—HEBREWS 6:14-19

Must I Really Have Everyone's Approval?

Who has believed our report?
And to whom has the arm of the LORD been
   revealed?
For He shall grow up before Him as a tender
   plant,
And as a root out of dry ground.
He has no form or comeliness;
And when we see Him,

There is no beauty that we should desire Him.
He is despised and rejected by men,
A Man of sorrows and acquainted with grief.
And we hid, as it were, our faces from Him;
He was despised, and we did not esteem
  Him.

—ISAIAH 53:1-3

"If the world hates you, you know that it hated Me before it hated you. If you were of the world, the world would love its own. Yet because you are not of the world, but I chose you out of the world, therefore the world hates you.

"Remember the word that I said to you, 'A servant is not greater than his master.' If they persecuted Me, they will also persecute you. If they kept My word, they will keep yours also.

"But all these things they will do to you for My name's sake, because they do not know Him who sent Me. If I had not come and spoken to them, they would have no sin, but now they have no excuse for their sin.

"He who hates Me hates My Father also. If I had not done among them the works which no one else did, they would have no sin; but now they have seen and also hated both Me and My Father.

"But this happened that the word might be fulfilled which is written in their law, 'They hated Me without a cause.'"

—JOHN 15:18-25

Will I Survive if Someone Is Angry with Me?

Blessed are you when they revile and persecute you, and say all kinds of evil against you falsely for My sake. Rejoice and be exceedingly glad, for great is your reward in heaven, for so they persecuted the prophets who were before you.

—MATTHEW 5:11–12

Beloved, do not think it strange concerning the fiery trial which is to try you, as though some strange thing happened to you; but rejoice to the extent that you partake of Christ's sufferings, that when His glory is revealed, you may also be glad with exceeding joy. If you are reproached for the name of Christ, blessed are you, for the Spirit of glory and of God rests upon you. On their part He is blasphemed, but on your part He is glorified.

But let none of you suffer as a murderer, a thief, an evildoer, or as a busybody in other people's matters. Yet if anyone suffers as a Christian, let him not be ashamed, but let him glorify God in this matter. For the time has come for judgment to begin at the house of God; and if it begins with us first, what will be the end of those who do not obey the gospel of God? Now

"If the righteous one is scarcely saved,
Where will the ungodly and the sinner
    appear?"

Therefore let those who suffer according to the will of God commit their souls to Him in doing good, as to a faithful Creator.

—1 PETER 4:12–19

Am I Really as Insignificant as I Feel?

"What is your servant, that you should look upon such a dead dog as I?"

—2 SAMUEL 9:8

"Do you thus deal with the LORD,
O foolish and unwise people?
Is He not your Father, who bought you?
Has He not made you and established you?
Remember the days of old,
Consider the years of many generations.
Ask your father, and he will show you;
Your elders, and they will tell you:
When the Most High divided their inheritance to the nations,
When He separated the sons of Adam,
He set the boundaries of the peoples
According to the number of the children of Israel.
For the LORD's portion is His people;
Jacob is the place of His inheritance.
He found him in a desert land
And in the wasteland, a howling wilderness;

He encircled him, He instructed him,
He kept him as the apple of His eye."
—DEUTERONOMY 32:6–10

Therefore He has mercy on whom He wills . . . that He might make known the riches of His glory on the vessels of mercy, which He had prepared beforehand for glory. . . . As He says also in Hosea:

"I will call them My people, who were not My people,
And her beloved, who was not beloved."
"And it shall come to pass in the place where it was said to them,
'You are not My people,'
There they will be called sons of the living God."
—ROMANS 9:18, 23, 25–26

Do I Really Have a Purpose in Life?

■ *I May Question Life's Meaning . . .*

"Why did I not die at birth?
Why did I not perish when I came from the
   womb?
Why did the knees receive me?
Or why the breasts, that I should nurse?
For now I would have lain still and been quiet,
I would have been asleep;
Then I would have been at rest."
—JOB 3:11–13

■ . . . *But God Gives Me Purpose*

Do you not know that you are the temple of God and that the Spirit of God dwells in you?

—1 CORINTHIANS 3:16

For we are His workmanship, created in Christ Jesus for good works, which God prepared beforehand that we should walk in them.

—EPHESIANS 2:10

Therefore, if anyone is in Christ, he is a new creation; old things have passed away; behold, all things have become new. Now all things are of God, who has reconciled us to Himself through Jesus Christ, and has given us the ministry of reconciliation, that is, that God was in Christ reconciling the world to Himself, not imputing their trespasses to them, and has committed to us the word of reconciliation. Therefore, we are ambassadors for Christ, as though God were pleading through us: we implore you on Christ's behalf, be reconciled to God.

—2 CORINTHIANS 5:17-20

That you may have a walk worthy of the Lord, fully pleasing Him, being fruitful in every good work and increasing in the knowledge of God; strengthened with all might, according to His glorious power, for all patience and longsuffering with joy; giving thanks to the Father who has qualified us to be partakers of the inheritance of the saints in the light.

—COLOSSIANS 1:10–12

"Go therefore and make disciples of all the nations, baptizing them in the name of the Father and of the Son and of the Holy Spirit, teaching them to observe all things that I have commanded you; and lo, I am with you always, even to the end of the age." Amen.

—MATTHEW 28:19–20

How Does God View Me?

Moses said to God, "Who am I . . . ?"

—EXODUS 3:11

■ God Sees My Potential

There has not arisen in Israel a prophet like Moses, whom the LORD knew face to face, in all the signs and wonders which the LORD sent him to do in the land of Egypt, before Pharaoh, before all his servants, and in all his land, and by all that mighty power and all the great terror which Moses performed in the sight of all Israel.

—DEUTERONOMY 34:10–12

■ God Sees Me as His Wonderful Creation

I will praise You, for I am fearfully and
    wonderfully made;

Marvelous are Your works,
And that my soul knows very well.
My frame was not hidden from You,
When I was made in secret,
And skillfully wrought in the lowest parts of
the earth.
Your eyes saw my substance, being yet
unformed.
And in Your book they all were written,
The days fashioned for me,
When as yet there were none of them.

—PSALM 139:14–16

Can I Learn to Stop Comparing Myself with Others?

For we dare not class ourselves or compare ourselves with those who commend themselves. But they, measuring themselves by themselves, and comparing themselves among themselves, are not wise. We, however, will not boast beyond measure, but within the limits of the sphere which God appointed us. . . . But "He who glories, let him glory in the LORD." For not he who commends himself is approved, but whom the Lord commends.

—2 CORINTHIANS 10:12–13, 17–18

For those who live according to the flesh set their minds on the things of the flesh, but those who live according to the Spirit, the things of the

Spirit. For to be carnally minded is death, but to be spiritually minded is life and peace. Because the carnal mind is enmity against God; for it is not subject to the law of God, nor indeed can be. So then, those who are in the flesh cannot please God.

—ROMANS 8:5-8

For Those Looking to Others for Happiness

"I can't be happy unless you are!" Yoshio wondered how he could possibly go through this all over again. It seemed that no matter what the situation, his wife, Sonia, found a way to blame him for her agitated states of mind. Yoshio often found himself trying to control his own moods, especially so-called "negative" feelings, so Sonia's attitude would be more upbeat. It was a real pressure trying to make sure she was happy, and he secretly felt they were both losing out on something—the interaction of complete personalities, the opportunity to relate as whole human beings. He wondered if it was worth it once again to paste on his phony smile and say: "No problem, honey."

Do you feed off other people's moods? Or can you find happiness within yourself and in your life with God?

People, Frail and Undependable, Will Let Me Down

"All flesh is grass,
And all its loveliness is like the flower of the
    field."

—ISAIAH 40:6b

You make his beauty melt away like a moth;
Surely every man is vapor.

—PSALM 39:11b

I said in my heart, "Concerning the condition of
the sons of men, God tests them, that they may
see that they themselves are like beasts."
For what happens to the sons of men also happens to beasts; one thing befalls them: as one dies,
so dies the other. Surely, they all have one breath;
man has no advantage over beasts, for all is vanity.
All go to one place: all are from the dust, and all
return to dust.

—ECCLESIASTES 3:18–20

Also do not take to heart everything people
    say,
Lest you hear your servant cursing you.
For many times, also, your own heart has
    known
That even you have cursed others.

—ECCLESIASTES 7:21–22

I returned and saw under the sun that—
The race is not to the swift,
Nor the battle to the strong,
Nor bread to the wise,
Nor riches to men of understanding,
Nor favor to men of skill;
But time and chance happen to them all.
For man also does not know his time:
Like fish taken in a cruel net,
Like birds caught in a snare,
So the sons of men are snared in an evil time,
When it falls suddenly upon them.

—ECCLESIASTES 9:11-12

. . . But God Will Not Disappoint Me

Now hope does not disappoint, because the love of God has been poured out in our hearts by the Holy Spirit who was given to us. For when we were still without strength, in due time Christ died for the ungodly. For scarcely for a righteous man will one die; yet perhaps for a good man someone would even dare to die. But God demonstrates His own love toward us, in that while we were still sinners, Christ died for us. Much more then, having now been justified by His blood, we shall be saved from wrath through Him.

—ROMANS 5:5-9

I know that whatever God does,
It shall be forever.
Nothing can be added to it,
And nothing taken from it.
God does it, that men should fear before Him.
—ECCLESIASTES 3:14

Remember now your Creator in the days of
    your youth,
Before the difficult days come,
And the years draw near when you say,
"I have no pleasure in them":
While the sun and the light,
The moon and the stars,
Are not darkened,
And the clouds do not return after the rain;
In the day when the keepers of the house
    tremble,
And the strong men bow down;
When the grinders cease because they are few,
And those that look through the windows
    grow dim;
When the doors are shut in the streets,
And the sound of grinding is low;
When one rises up at the sound of a bird,
And all the daughters of music are brought
    low;
Also they are afraid of height,
And of terrors in the way;
When the almond tree blossoms,
The grasshopper is a burden,

And desire fails.
For man goes to his eternal home,
And the mourners go about the streets.
Remember your Creator before the silver cord
is loosed,
Or the golden bowl is broken,
Or the pitcher shattered at the fountain,
Or the wheel broken at the well.
Then the dust will return to the earth as it
was,
And the spirit will return to God who gave it.
—ECCLESIASTES 12:1-7

I Must Take Care of Myself

■ Allowing Myself to Rest

The apostles gathered to Jesus and told Him all things, both what they had done and what they had taught. And He said to them, "Come aside by yourselves to a deserted place and rest a while." For there were many coming and going, and they did not even have time to eat. So they departed to a deserted place in the boat by themselves.

—MARK 6:30-32

Six days you shall do your work, and on the
seventh day you shall rest.

—EXODUS 23:12a

■ Making Time for Exercise

When you walk, your steps will not be
   hindered,
And when you run, you will not stumble.

—PROVERBS 4:12

For by You I can run against a troop;
By my God I can leap over a wall.

—2 SAMUEL 22:30

He gives power to the weak,
And to those who have no might He increases
   strength.
Even the youths shall faint and be weary,
And the young men shall utterly fall,
But those who wait on the LORD
Shall renew their strength;
They shall mount up with wings like eagles,
They shall run and not be weary,
They shall walk and not faint.

—ISAIAH 40:29–31

I beseech you therefore, brethren, by the mercies of God, that you present your bodies a living
sacrifice, holy, acceptable to God, which is your
reasonable service.

—ROMANS 12:1

Or do you not know that your body is the temple of the Holy Spirit who is in you, whom you

have from God, and you are not your own? For you were bought at a price; therefore glorify God in your body and in your spirit, which are God's.
—1 CORINTHIANS 6:19, 20

For our citizenship is in heaven, from which we also eagerly wait for the Savior, the Lord Jesus Christ, who will transform our lowly body that it may be conformed to His glorious body, according to the working by which He is able even to subdue all things to Himself.

—PHILIPPIANS 3:20, 21

■ Watching My Nutrition

There is nothing better for a man than that he should eat and drink, and that his soul should enjoy good in his labor. This also, I saw, was from the hand of God.

—ECCLESIASTES 2:24

. . . and also that every man should eat and drink and enjoy the good of all his labor—it is the gift of God.

—ECCLESIASTES 3:13

Here is what I have seen: It is good and fitting for one to eat and drink, and to enjoy the good of all his labor in which he toils under the sun all the days of his life which God gives him; for it is his heritage. As for every man to whom God has

given riches and wealth, and given him power to
eat of it, to receive his heritage and rejoice in his
labor—this is the gift of God.

—ECCLESIASTES 5:18–19

■ Getting Enough Sleep

I lay down and slept;
I awoke, for the LORD sustained me.

—PSALM 3:5

Meditate within your heart on your bed, and
    be still.
Offer the sacrifices of righteousness,
And put your trust in the LORD.
There are many who say,
"Who will show us any good?"
LORD, lift up the light of Your countenance
    upon us.
You have put gladness in my heart,
More than in the season that their grain and
    wine increased.
I will both lie down in peace, and sleep;
For You alone, O LORD, make me dwell in
    safety.

—PSALM 4:4b–8

Now when [Jesus] got into a boat, His disciples
followed Him. And suddenly a great tempest
arose on the sea, so that the boat was covered with
the waves. But He was asleep.

—MATTHEW 8:23–24

■ Being with Friends

Faithful are the wounds of a friend,
But the kisses of an enemy are deceitful. . . .
Ointment and perfume delight the heart,
And the sweetness of a man's friend does so
    by hearty counsel.
Do not forsake your own friend or your
    father's friend,
Nor go to your brother's house in the day of
    your calamity;
For better is a neighbor nearby than a brother
    far away.

—PROVERBS 27:6, 9–10

Comfort each other and edify one another, just as you also are doing. . . . Now we exhort you, brethren, warn those who are unruly, comfort the fainthearted, uphold the weak, be patient with all.
—1 THESSALONIANS 5:11, 14

Not forsaking the assembling of ourselves together, as is the manner of some, but exhorting one another, and so much the more as you see the Day approaching.
—HEBREWS 10:25

■ Seeking Daily Help from God

I will lift up my eyes to the hills—
From whence comes my help?
My help comes from the LORD,

Who made heaven and earth.
He will not allow your foot to be moved;
He who keeps you will not slumber.
Behold, He who keeps Israel
Shall neither slumber nor sleep.
The LORD is your keeper;
The LORD is your shade at your right hand.
The sun shall not strike you by day,
Nor the moon by night.
The LORD shall preserve you from all evil;
He shall preserve your soul.
The LORD shall preserve your going out and
    your coming in
From this time forth, and even forevermore.
                              —PSALM 121:1–8

O God, do not be far from me;
O my God, make haste to help me!
Let them be confounded and consumed
Who are adversaries of my life;
Let them be covered with reproach and
    dishonor
Who seek my hurt.
But I will hope continually,
And will praise You yet more and more.
My mouth shall tell of Your righteousness
And Your salvation all the day,
For I do not know their limits.
I will go in the strength of the Lord GOD;
I will make mention of Your righteousness, of
    Yours only.
O God, You have taught me from my youth;

And to this day I declare Your wondrous
  works.
Now also when I am old and grayheaded,
O God, do not forsake me,
Until I declare Your strength to this
  generation,
Your power to everyone who is to come.
Also Your righteousness, O God, is very high,
You who have done great things;
O God, who is like You?

PSALM 71:12–19

Seeing then that we have a great High Priest
who has passed through the heavens, Jesus the
Son of God, let us hold fast our confession. For we
do not have a High Priest who cannot sympathize
with our weaknesses, but was in all points
tempted as we are, yet without sin. Let us therefore come boldly to the throne of grace, that we
may obtain mercy and find grace to help in time of
need.

—HEBREWS 4:14–16

■ Opening Up to God's Care

The LORD is your keeper;
The LORD is your shade at your right hand.
The sun shall not strike you by day,
Nor the moon by night.
The LORD shall preserve you from all evil;
He shall preserve your soul.

The LORD shall preserve your going out and
   your coming in
From this time forth, and even forevermore.
—PSALM 121:5-8

For thus says the Lord GOD: "Indeed I Myself
will search for My sheep and seek them out. As a
shepherd seeks out his flock on the day he is
among his scattered sheep, so will I seek out My
sheep and deliver them from all the places where
they were scattered on a cloudy and dark day.
"And I will bring them out from the peoples and
gather them from the countries, and will bring
them to their own land; I will feed them on the
mountains of Israel, in the valleys and in all the
inhabited places of the country. I will feed them in
good pasture, and their fold shall be on the high
mountains of Israel. There they shall lie down in a
good fold and feed in rich pasture on the mountains of Israel. I will feed My flock, and I will make
them lie down," says the Lord GOD.
"I will seek what was lost and bring back what
was driven away, bind up the broken and
strengthen what was sick; but I will destroy the fat
and the strong, and feed them in judgment."
—EZEKIEL 34:11–16

Eternal Things Provide My Lasting Happiness

Jesus said to him, "'You shall love the LORD your God with all your heart, with all your soul, and with all your mind.'"

—MATTHEW 22:37

If then you were raised with Christ, seek those things which are above, where Christ is, sitting at the right hand of God. Set your mind on things above, not on things on the earth. For you died, and your life is hidden with Christ in God. When Christ who is our life appears, then you also will appear with Him in glory.

—COLOSSIANS 3:1-4

Finally, brethren, whatever things are true, whatever things are noble, whatever things are just, whatever things are pure, whatever things are lovely, whatever things are of good report, if there is any virtue and if there is anything praiseworthy—meditate on these things.

—PHILIPPIANS 4:8

For Those Feeling Overly Responsible

Marsha could hardly believe it, but once again she was sitting at the kitchen table, poring over ninth-grade algebra problems. She was an adult, doing her son's homework again! But suppose Jason were to flunk the class? Then what? How could she face that kind of failure? Besides, was it really Jason's fault that he did not get along with the math teacher? It felt to Marsha, vaguely, as though it was mostly her own fault.

Here's the codependent need to be responsible for everything: Taking on everybody's problems; feeling guilty about not doing enough for others; knowing I should be able to help. When somebody's hurting, it's my fault. In those cases I am judge and jury. The verdict is always against me. Only I can decide to suspend sentence. . . .

Are You Feeling the Need to Rescue Others?

So Moses returned to the LORD and said, "Lord, why have You brought trouble on this people? Why is it You have sent me? For since I came to Pharaoh to speak in Your name, he has done evil to this people; neither have You delivered Your people at all."

—EXODUS 5:22–23

And Moses spoke before the LORD, saying, "The children of Israel have not heeded me. How then shall Pharaoh heed me? . . ." Then the LORD spoke to Moses and Aaron, and gave them a command for the children of Israel and for Pharaoh king of Egypt, to bring the children of Israel out of the land of Egypt.

—EXODUS 6:12–13

―――――――――■■――――――――

. . . But God is the True Rescuer

So the LORD saved Israel that day out of the hand of the Egyptians, and Israel saw the Egyptians dead on the seashore. Thus Israel saw the great work which the LORD had done in Egypt; so the people feared the LORD, and believed the LORD and His servant Moses.

—EXODUS 14:30–31

Then Moses and the children of Israel sang this song to the LORD, and spoke, saying:

"I will sing to the LORD,
For He has triumphed gloriously!
The horse and its rider
He has thrown into the sea!
The LORD is my strength and song,
And He has become my salvation;
He is my God, and I will praise Him;
My father's God, and I will exalt Him.
The LORD is a man of war;
The LORD is His name.
Pharaoh's chariots and his army He has cast
    into the sea;
His chosen captains also are drowned in the
    Red Sea.
The depths have covered them;
They sank to the bottom like a stone.
Your right hand, O LORD, has become glorious
    in power;
Your right hand, O LORD, has dashed the
    enemy in pieces.
And in the greatness of Your excellence
You have overthrown those who rose against
    You;
You sent forth Your wrath;
It consumed them like stubble.
And with the blast of Your nostrils
The waters were gathered together;
The floods stood upright like a heap;
The depths congealed in the heart of the sea.

The enemy said, 'I will pursue, I will
   overtake, I will divide the spoil;
My desire shall be satisfied on them. I will
   draw my sword,
My hand shall destroy them.'
You blew with Your wind,
The sea covered them;
They sank like lead in the mighty waters.
Who is like You, O LORD, among the gods?
Who is like You, glorious in holiness,
Fearful in praises, doing wonders? . . .
The LORD shall reign forever and ever."

—EXODUS 15:1–11, 18

Are You Feeling Like a Martyr with Eyes on Another?

Now it happened as they went that He entered a
certain village; and a certain woman named Martha welcomed Him into her house. And she had a
sister called Mary, who also sat at Jesus' feet and
heard His word. But Martha was distracted with
much serving, and she approached Him and said,
"Lord, do You not care that my sister has left me to
serve alone? Therefore tell her to help me."

And Jesus answered and said to her, "Martha,
Martha, you are worried and troubled about many
things. But one thing is needed, and Mary has
chosen that good part, which will not be taken
away from her."

—LUKE 10:38–42

. . . But True Martyrdom Is Unselfish with Eyes on the Lord

"Which of the prophets did your fathers not persecute? And they killed those who foretold the coming of the Just One, of whom you now have become the betrayers and murderers, who have received the law by the direction of angels and have not kept it."

When they heard these things they were cut to the heart, and they gnashed at him with their teeth. But he, being full of the Holy Spirit, gazed into heaven and saw the glory of God, and Jesus standing at the right hand of God, and said, "Look! I see the heavens opened and the Son of Man standing at the right hand of God!"

Then they cried out with a loud voice, stopped their ears, and ran at him with one accord; and they cast him out of the city and stoned him. And the witnesses laid down their clothes at the feet of a young man named Saul. And they stoned Stephen as he was calling on God and saying, "Lord Jesus, receive my spirit."

—ACTS 7:52–59

Are You Willing to Set Boundaries?

■ *Setting Boundaries in Relationships*

"If your brother sins against you, go and tell him his fault between you and him alone. If he hears you, you have gained your brother. But if he will not hear, take with you one or two more, that 'by the mouth of two or three witnesses every word may be established.'

"And if he refuses to hear them, tell it to the church. But if he refuses even to hear the church, let him be to you like a heathen and a tax collector."

—MATTHEW 18:15–17

Therefore, putting away lying, each one speak truth with his neighbor, for we are members of one another.

—EPHESIANS 4:25

■ Setting Boundaries in Sexual Matters

"I have made a covenant with my eyes;
Why then should I look upon a young
    woman? . . .
If my heart has been enticed by a woman,
Or if I have lurked at my neighbor's door,
Then let my wife grind for another,
And let others bow down over her.
For that would be wickedness;
Yes, it would be iniquity worthy of judgment.
For that would be a fire that consumes to
    destruction,
And would root out all my increase."

—JOB 31:1, 9–12

For at the window of my house
I looked through my lattice,
And saw among the simple,
I perceived among the youths,
A young man devoid of understanding,
Passing along the street near her corner;
And he took the path to her house
In the twilight, in the evening,
In the black and dark night.
And there a woman met him,
With the attire of a harlot, and a crafty
    heart. . . .
"Come, let us take our fill of love until
    morning;
Let us delight ourselves with love.
For my husband is not at home;
He has gone on a long journey;
He has taken a bag of money with him,
And will come home on the appointed day."
With her enticing speech she caused him to
    yield,
With her flattering lips she seduced him.
Immediately he went after her, as an ox goes
    to the slaughter,
Or as a fool to the correction of the stocks.
                —PROVERBS 7:6–10, 18–22

■ Setting Boundaries in Financial Matters

Now Jesus sat opposite the treasury and saw
how the people put money into the treasury. And
many who were rich put in much. Then one poor

widow came and threw in two mites, which make a quadrans. So He called His disciples to Him and said to them, "Assuredly, I say to you that this poor widow has put in more than all those who have given to the treasury; for they all put in out of their abundance, but she out of her poverty put in all that she had, her whole livelihood."

—MARK 12:41–44

"Do not fear, little flock, for it is your Father's good pleasure to give you the kingdom. Sell what you have and give alms; provide yourselves money bags which do not grow old, a treasure in the heavens that does not fail, where no thief approaches nor moth destroys. For where your treasure is, there your heart will be also."

—LUKE 12:32–34

But godliness with contentment is great gain. For we brought nothing into this world, and it is certain we can carry nothing out. And having food and clothing, with these we shall be content. But those who desire to be rich fall into temptation and a snare, and into many foolish and harmful lusts which drown men in destruction and perdition. For the love of money is a root of all kinds of evil, for which some have strayed from the faith in their greediness, and pierced themselves through with many sorrows. But you, O man of God, flee these things and pursue righteousness, godliness, faith, love, patience, gentleness.

—1 TIMOTHY 6:6–11

■ *Setting Boundaries with Food and Drink*

For none of us lives to himself, and no one dies to himself. For if we live, we live to the Lord; and if we die, we die to the Lord. Therefore, whether we live or die, we are the Lord's. For to this end Christ died and rose and lived again, that He might be Lord of both the dead and the living. . . .

So then each of us shall give account of himself to God. Therefore let us not judge one another anymore, but rather resolve this, not to put a stumbling block or a cause to fall in our brother's way.

I know and am convinced by the Lord Jesus that there is nothing unclean of itself; but to him who considers anything to be unclean, to him it is unclean. . . . For the kingdom of God is not food and drink, but righteousness and peace and joy in the Holy Spirit. . . .

It is good neither to eat meat nor drink wine nor do anything by which your brother stumbles or is offended or is made weak. Do you have faith? Have it to yourself before God. Happy is he who does not condemn himself in what he approves.

—ROMANS 14:7–9, 12–14, 17, 21–22

Are You Able to Say Good-Bye?

■ *Departing from Father and Mother*

And the LORD God caused a deep sleep to fall on Adam, and he slept; and He took one of his ribs, and closed up the flesh in its place. Then the rib which the LORD God had taken from man He made into a woman, and He brought her to the man. And Adam said:

"This is now bone of my bones
And flesh of my flesh;
She shall be called Woman,
Because she was taken out of Man."

Therefore a man shall leave his father and mother and be joined to his wife, and they shall become one flesh.

—GENESIS 2:21-24

Now after John was put in prison, Jesus came to Galilee, preaching the gospel of the kingdom of God, and saying, "The time is fulfilled, and the kingdom of God is at hand. Repent, and believe in the gospel."

And as He walked by the Sea of Galilee, He saw Simon and Andrew his brother casting a net into the sea; for they were fishermen. Then Jesus said to them, "Come after Me, and I will make you become fishers of men."

And they immediately left their nets and followed Him. When He had gone a little farther from there, He saw James the son of Zebedee, and John his brother, who also were in the boat mending their nets. And immediately He called them, and they left their father Zebedee in the boat with the hired servants, and went after Him.

—MARK 1:14-20

■ *'Leaving' Home and Family of Origin*

Now it happened as they journeyed on the road, that someone said to Him, "Lord, I will follow You wherever You go."

And Jesus said to him, "Foxes have holes and birds of the air have nests, but the Son of Man has nowhere to lay His head."

Then He said to another, "Follow Me."

But he said, "Lord, let me first go and bury my father."

Jesus said to him, "Let the dead bury their own dead, but you go and preach the kingdom of God."

—LUKE 9:57–60

■ *Following Christ, Your Greatest Responsibility*

Then He said to him, "A certain man gave a great supper and invited many, and sent his servant at supper time to say to those who were invited, 'Come, for all things are now ready.'

"But they all with one accord began to make excuses. The first said to him, 'I have bought a piece of ground, and I must go and see it. I ask you to have me excused.'

"And another said, 'I have bought five yoke of oxen, and I am going to test them. I ask you to have me excused.'

"Still another said, 'I have married a wife, and therefore I cannot come.' So that servant came and reported these things to his master.

"Then the master of the house, being angry, said to his servant, 'Go out quickly into the streets and lanes of the city, and bring in here the poor and the maimed and the lame and the blind.'

"And the servant said, 'Master, it is done as you commanded, and still there is room.'

"Then the master said to the servant, 'Go out into the highways and hedges, and compel them to come in, that my house may be filled. For I say to you that none of those men who were invited shall taste my supper.'" . . .

And He turned and said to them, "If anyone comes to Me and does not hate his father and mother, wife and children, brothers and sisters, yes, and his own life also, he cannot be My disciple."

—LUKE 14:16–25a, 26

Are You Ready to Ask for Help?

I will lift up my eyes to the hills—
From whence comes my help?
My help comes from the LORD,
Who made heaven and earth.
He will not allow your foot to be moved;
He who keeps you will not slumber.
Behold, He who keeps Israel
Shall neither slumber nor sleep.
The LORD is your keeper;
The LORD is your shade at your right hand.
The sun shall not strike you by day,

Nor the moon by night.
The LORD shall preserve you from all evil;
He shall preserve your soul.
The LORD shall preserve your going out and
  your coming in
From this time forth, and even forevermore.

—PSALM 121:1–8

CHAPTER 6

For Those Suffering Imbalance in Relationships

Which will it be: "I can't live without you," or: "I can make it on my own without you or anyone else"? Those appear to be the only options facing the codependent person. It's all or nothing. Complete dependence or total independence. In this scheme of things, relationships get severely out of balance.

The Bible shows us that our God is a God of relationships, who bases His dealings with us on a covenant that balances love, respect, and justice. If we're seeking direction in handling our relationships, we need to look no further than the promises of the one who created us to experience eternal joy in His personal presence.

Relationships in Christ's Kingdom

■ *Display Attitudes that Bring God's Blessing*

Then He opened His mouth and taught them, saying:

"Blessed are the poor in spirit,
For theirs is the kingdom of heaven.
Blessed are those who mourn,
For they shall be comforted.
Blessed are the meek,
For they shall inherit the earth.
Blessed are those who hunger and thirst for
    righteousness,
For they shall be filled.
Blessed are the merciful,
For they shall obtain mercy.
Blessed are the pure in heart,
For they shall see God.
Blessed are the peacemakers,
For they shall be called sons of God.
Blessed are those who are persecuted for
    righteousness' sake,
For theirs is the kingdom of heaven.
Blessed are you when they revile and
    persecute you, and say all kinds of evil
    against you falsely for My sake. Rejoice and
    be exceedingly glad, for great is your reward
    in heaven, for so they persecuted the
    prophets who were before you."

—MATTHEW 5:2–12

■ Maintain the Proper Heart Attitude

Hatred

"You have heard that it was said to those of old, 'You shall not murder, and whoever murders will be in danger of the judgment.' But I say to you that whoever is angry with his brother without a cause shall be in danger of the judgment. And whoever says to his brother, 'Raca!' shall be in danger of the council. But whoever says, 'You fool!' shall be in danger of hell fire.

"Therefore if you bring your gift to the altar, and there remember that your brother has something against you, leave your gift there before the altar, and go your way. First be reconciled to your brother, and then come and offer your gift.

"Agree with your adversary quickly, while you are on the way with him, lest your adversary deliver you to the judge, the judge hand you over to the officer, and you be thrown into prison. Assuredly, I say to you, you will by no means get out of there till you have paid the last penny."

—MATTHEW 5:21–26

Adultery

"You have heard that it was said to those of old, 'You shall not commit adultery.' But I say to you that whoever looks at a woman to lust for her has already committed adultery with her in his heart."

—MATTHEW 5:27–28

Fighting

"You have heard that it was said, 'An eye for an eye and a tooth for a tooth.' But I tell you not to resist an evil person. But whoever slaps you on your right cheek, turn the other to him also. If anyone wants to sue you and take away your tunic, let him have your cloak also. And whoever compels you to go one mile, go with him two.

"Give to him who asks you, and from him who wants to borrow from you do not turn away."

—MATTHEW 5:38–42

Enemies

"You have heard that it was said, 'You shall love your neighbor and hate your enemy.' But I say to you, love your enemies, bless those who curse you, do good to those who hate you, and pray for those who spitefully use you and persecute you, that you may be sons of your Father in heaven; for He makes His sun rise on the evil and on the good, and sends rain on the just and on the unjust.

"For if you love those who love you, what reward have you? Do not even the tax collectors do the same? And if you greet your brethren only, what do you do more than others? Do not even the tax collectors do so?"

—MATTHEW 5:43–47

Relationships in the Church

■ *Love Your Brother*

In this the children of God and the children of the devil are manifest: Whoever does not practice righteousness is not of God, nor is he who does not love his brother. For this is the message that you heard from the beginning, that we should love one another, not as Cain who was of the wicked one and murdered his brother. And why did he murder him? Because his works were evil and his brother's righteous.

Do not marvel, my brethren, if the world hates you. We know that we have passed from death to life, because we love the brethren. He who does not love his brother abides in death. Whoever hates his brother is a murderer, and you know that no murderer has eternal life abiding in him.

—1 JOHN 3:10–15

For I say, through the grace given to me, to everyone who is among you, not to think of himself more highly than he ought to think, but to think soberly, as God has dealt to each one a measure of faith. For as we have many members in one body, but all the members do not have the same function, so we, being many, are one body in Christ, and individually members of one another.

Having then gifts differing according to the grace that is given to us, let us use them: if prophecy, let us prophesy in proportion to our faith; or ministry, let us use it in our ministering; he who teaches, in teaching; he who exhorts, in exhortation; he who gives, with liberality; he who leads, with diligence; he who shows mercy, with cheerfulness.

Let love be without hypocrisy. Abhor what is evil. Cling to what is good. Be kindly affectionate to one another with brotherly love, in honor giving preference to one another.

—ROMANS 12:3–10

■ *Do Not Judge Your Brother*

Hatred Leads to Violence

Now Abel was a keeper of sheep, but Cain was a tiller of the ground. And in the process of time it came to pass that Cain brought an offering of the fruit of the ground to the LORD. Abel also brought of the firstlings of his flock and of their fat. And the LORD respected Abel and his offering, but He did not respect Cain and his offering.

And Cain was very angry, and his countenance fell. So the LORD said to Cain, "Why are you angry? And why has your countenance fallen? If you do well, will you not be accepted? And if you do not do well, sin lies at the door. And its desire is for you, but you should rule over it."

Now Cain talked with Abel his brother; and it came to pass, when they were in the field, that Cain rose against Abel his brother and killed him.

Then the LORD said to Cain, "Where is Abel your brother?"

And he said, "I do not know. Am I my brother's keeper?"

—GENESIS 4:2b–9

Humility Leads to God's Uplifting

Humble yourselves in the sight of the Lord, and He will lift you up. Do not speak evil of one another, brethren. He who speaks evil of a brother and judges his brother, speaks evil of the law and judges the law. But if you judge the law, you are not a doer of the law but a judge. There is one Lawgiver, who is able to save and to destroy. Who are you to judge another?

—JAMES 4:10–12

■ Function in Unity, as Members of One Body

For as the body is one and has many members, but all the members of that one body, being many, are one body, so also is Christ. For by one Spirit we were all baptized into one body—whether Jews or Greeks, whether slaves or free—and have all been made to drink into one Spirit. For in fact the body is not one member but many.

If the foot should say, "Because I am not a hand, I am not of the body," is it therefore not of the body? And if the ear should say, "Because I am not an eye, I am not of the body," is it therefore not of the body?

If the whole body were an eye, where would be

the hearing? If the whole were hearing, where would be the smelling? But now God has set the members, each one of them, in the body just as He pleased. And if they were all one member, where would the body be?

But now indeed there are many members, yet one body. And the eye cannot say to the hand, "I have no need of you"; nor again the head to the feet, "I have no need of you." No, much rather, those members of the body which seem to be weaker are necessary. And those members of the body which we think to be less honorable, on these we bestow greater honor; and our unpresentable parts have greater modesty, but our presentable parts have no need.

But God composed the body, having given greater honor to that part which lacks it, that there should be no schism in the body, but that the members should have the same care for one another. And if one member suffers, all the members suffer with it; or if one member is honored, all the members rejoice with it.

—1 CORINTHIANS 12:12–26

■ Serve One Another

So when He had washed their feet, taken His garments, and sat down again, He said to them, "Do you know what I have done to you? You call me Teacher and Lord, and you say well, for so I am. If I then, your Lord and Teacher, have washed your feet, you also ought to wash one another's feet. For I have given you an example, that you should do as I have done to you.

"Most assuredly, I say to you, a servant is not greater than his master; nor is he who is sent greater than he who sent him. If you know these things, happy are you if you do them."

—JOHN 13:12–17

Relationships in Marriage and Family

Now to the married I command, yet not I but the Lord: A wife is not to depart from her husband. But even if she does depart, let her remain unmarried or be reconciled to her husband. And a husband is not to divorce his wife.

But to the rest I, not the Lord, say: If any brother has a wife who does not believe, and she is willing to live with him, let him not divorce her. And a woman who has a husband who does not believe, if he is willing to live with her, let her not divorce him. For the unbelieving husband is sanctified by the wife, and the unbelieving wife is sanctified by the husband; otherwise your children would be unclean, but now they are holy.

But if the unbeliever departs, let him depart; a brother or a sister is not under bondage in such cases. But God has called us to peace. For how do you know, O wife, whether you will save your husband? Or how do you know, O husband, whether you will save your wife?

—1 CORINTHIANS 7:10–16

Are you bound to a wife? Do not seek to be loosed. Are you loosed from a wife? Do not seek a wife. But even if you do marry, you have not sinned; and if a virgin marries, she has not sinned. Nevertheless such will have trouble in the flesh, but I would spare you.

—1 CORINTHIANS 7:27–28

■ Don't Be Unequally Yoked

Do not be unequally yoked together with unbelievers. For what fellowship has righteousness with lawlessness? And what communion has light with darkness? And what accord has Christ with Belial? Or what part has a believer with an unbeliever? And what agreement has the temple of God with idols? For you are the temple of the living God. As God has said:

"I will dwell in them
And walk among them.
I will be their God,
And they shall be My people."
Therefore
"Come out from among them
And be separate, says the Lord.
Do not touch what is unclean,
And I will receive you."

—2 CORINTHIANS 6:14–17

■ *Be a Good Wife/Mother*

Submitting to one another in the fear of God. Wives, submit to your own husbands, as to the Lord. For the husband is head of the wife, as also Christ is head of the church; and He is the Savior of the body. Therefore, just as the church is subject to Christ, so let the wives be to their own husbands in everything.

—EPHESIANS 5:21–24

She perceives that her merchandise is good,
And her lamp does not go out by night.
She stretches out her hands to the distaff,
And her hand holds the spindle.
She extends her hand to the poor,
Yes, she reaches out her hands to the needy.
She is not afraid of snow for her household,
For all her household is clothed with scarlet.
She makes tapestry for herself;
Her clothing is fine linen and purple.
Her husband is known in the gates,
When he sits among the elders of the land.
She makes linen garments and sells them,
And supplies sashes for the merchants.
Strength and honor are her clothing;
She shall rejoice in time to come.
She opens her mouth with wisdom,
And on her tongue is the law of kindness.
She watches over the ways of her household,
And does not eat the bread of idleness.

Her children rise up and call her blessed;
Her husband also, and he praises her:
"Many daughters have done well,
But you excel them all."

—PROVERBS 31:18–29

■ Be a Good Husband/Father

Submitting to one another in the fear of God.

—EPHESIANS 5:21

Husbands, love your wives, just as Christ also loved the church and gave Himself for it, that He might sanctify and cleanse it with the washing of water by the word, that He might present it to Himself a glorious church, not having spot or wrinkle or any such thing, but that it should be holy and without blemish. So husbands ought to love their own wives as their own bodies; he who loves his wife loves himself. For no one ever hated his own flesh, but nourishes and cherishes it, just as the Lord does the church. For we are members of His body, of His flesh and of His bones. "For this reason a man shall leave his father and mother and be joined to his wife, and the two shall become one flesh." This is a great mystery, but I speak concerning Christ and the church. Nevertheless let each one of you in particular so love his own wife as himself.

—EPHESIANS 5:25–33

Fathers, do not provoke your children, lest
they become discouraged.

—COLOSSIANS 3:21

Relationships in General

■ *Use Effective Communication for Peaceful Relating*

A soft answer turns away wrath,
But a harsh word stirs up anger.
The tongue of the wise uses knowledge
rightly,
But the mouth of fools pours forth
foolishness. . . .
A wholesome tongue is a tree of life,
But perverseness in it breaks the spirit.

—PROVERBS 15:1–2, 4

He who heeds the word wisely will find good,
And whoever trusts in the LORD, happy is he.
The wise in heart will be called prudent,
And sweetness of the lips increases learning.
Understanding is a wellspring of life to him
who has it.
But the correction of fools is folly.
The heart of the wise teaches his mouth,
And adds learning to his lips.
Pleasant words are like a honeycomb,
Sweetness to the soul and health to the bones.

—PROVERBS 16:20–24

A word fitly spoken is like apples of gold
In settings of silver.

—PROVERBS 25:11

"But let your 'Yes' be 'Yes,' and your 'No,' 'No.'
For whatever is more than these is from the evil
one."

—MATTHEW 5:37

■ Pursue the Ultimate Goal: Self-Giving Love

Though I speak with the tongues of men and of
angels, but have not love, I have become as sounding brass or a clanging cymbal. And though I have
the gift of prophecy, and understand all mysteries
and all knowledge, and though I have all faith, so
that I could remove mountains, but have not love,
I am nothing. And though I bestow all my goods
to feed the poor, and though I give my body to be
burned, but have not love, it profits me nothing.

Love suffers long and is kind; love does not
envy; love does not parade itself, is not puffed up;
does not behave rudely, does not seek its own, is
not provoked, thinks no evil; does not rejoice in
iniquity, but rejoices in the truth; bears all things,
believes all things, hopes all things, endures all
things. Love never fails.

But whether there are prophecies, they will fail;
whether there are tongues, they will cease;
whether there is knowledge, it will vanish away.
For we know in part and we prophesy in part. But

when that which is perfect has come, then that which is in part will be done away.

When I was a child, I spoke as a child, I understood as a child, I thought as a child; but when I became a man, I put away childish things. For now we see in a mirror, dimly, but then face to face. Now I know in part, but then I shall know just as I also am known.

And now abide faith, hope, love, these three; but the greatest of these is love.

—1 CORINTHIANS 13:1–13

For Those Clinging to Denial

The psychologist had heard it so often: "Actually, Doctor, my childhood was quite happy. I just don't understand why I'm having all these problems." The counselor knows, or course, that in just a few short months the client's story will sound quite different. Memories will have become more vivid, tears will have flowed, pain will have been touched. "All these problems" will not only be in the present but will have become linked to the pain of the past.

What capacity we have for denial! As codependents, we often do not recognize childhood trauma as abnormal and abusive until we get help to see it for what it was. Denial "saved" us, helped us survive our childhood love-hunger. Making excuses for parents' behavior became less frightening and sad than seeing ourselves as victims without the means of self-protection.

Blaming is not the solution, however. We

can't change the past and we certainly can't change the persons who have hurt us (they probably did the best they could). We can only change ourselves, with God's help. So let us start there: Admitting our own faults and the roles we ourselves played in contributing to patterns of deprivation. Then we can trust God to move us toward healthy personhood.

I Can't Deny It: I Really Have Been Hurt!

Woe is me for my hurt!
My wound is severe.
But I say, "Truly this is an infirmity,
And I must bear it."

—JEREMIAH 10:19

■ God Knows My Inner Pain

O my soul, my soul!
I am pained in my very heart!
My heart makes a noise in me;
I cannot hold my peace.

—JEREMIAH 4:19

Why is my pain perpetual
And my wound incurable,
Which refuses to be healed?

Will You surely be to me like an unreliable
    stream,
As waters that fail?

—JEREMIAH 15:18

When I thought how to understand this,
It was too painful for me.

—PSALM 73:16

For my iniquities have gone over my head;
Like a heavy burden they are too heavy for
    me.
My wounds are foul and festering
Because of my foolishness.
I am troubled, I am bowed down greatly;
I go mourning all the day long.
For my loins are full of inflammation,
And there is no soundness in my flesh.
I am feeble and severely broken;
I groan because of the turmoil of my heart.

—PSALM 38:4–8

He has made His wonderful works to be
    remembered;
The LORD is gracious and full of compassion.

—PSALM 111:4

The LORD is gracious and full of compassion,
Slow to anger and great in mercy.

—PSALM 145:8

Though He causes grief,
Yet He will show compassion
According to the multitude of His mercies.

—LAMENTATIONS 3:32

■ God Sees My Tears

"Remember now, O LORD, I pray, how I have walked before You in truth and with a loyal heart, and have done what was good in Your sight." And Hezekiah wept bitterly.

Then it happened, before Isaiah had gone out into the middle court, that the word of the LORD came to him, saying, "Return and tell Hezekiah the leader of My people, 'Thus says the LORD, the God of David your father: "I have heard your prayer, I have seen your tears; surely I will heal you."'"

—2 KINGS 20:3–5a

■ God Hears My Inner Groanings

Therefore [the Egyptians] set taskmasters over [the Israelites] to afflict them with their burdens. . . . So the Egyptians made the children of Israel serve with rigor. And they made their lives bitter with hard bondage—in mortar, in brick, and in all manner of service in the field. All their service in which they made them serve was with rigor. . . .

Now it happened in the process of time that the king of Egypt died. Then the children of Israel groaned because of the bondage, and they cried out; and their cry came up to God because of the bondage. So God heard their groaning, and God remembered His covenant with Abraham, with Isaac, and with Jacob. And God looked upon the children of Israel, and God acknowledged them.

—EXODUS 1:11, 13–14; 2:23–25

■ God Provides in My Wilderness of Affliction

"You saw the affliction of our fathers in Egypt,
And heard their cry by the Red Sea.
You showed signs and wonders against Pharaoh,
Against all his servants,
And against all the people of his land.
For You knew that they acted proudly against them.
So You made a name for Yourself, as it is this day.
And You divided the sea before them,
So that they went through the midst of the sea on the dry land;
And their persecutors You threw into the deep,
As a stone into the mighty waters.
Moreover You led them by day with a cloudy pillar,
And by night with a pillar of fire,

To give them light on the road
Which they should travel.
You came down also on Mount Sinai,
And spoke with them from heaven,
And gave them just ordinances and true laws,
Good statutes and commandments.
You made known to them Your holy Sabbath,
And commanded them precepts, statutes and laws,
By the hand of Moses Your servant.
You gave them bread from heaven for their hunger,
And brought them water out of the rock for their thirst,
And told them to go in to possess the land
Which You had sworn to give them. . . .
In Your manifold mercies
You did not forsake them in the wilderness.
The pillar of the cloud did not depart from them by day,
To lead them on the road;
Nor the pillar of fire by night,
To show them light,
And the way they should go.
You also gave Your good Spirit to instruct them,
And did not withhold Your manna from their mouth,
And gave them water for their thirst."

—NEHEMIAH 9:9–15, 19–20

I Can't Deny It: I Also Have Sinned

■ *Opening to Self-Examination*

Examine yourselves as to whether you are in the faith. Prove yourselves. Do you not know yourselves, that Jesus Christ is in you?—unless indeed you are disqualified.

—2 CORINTHIANS 13:5

Now the works of the flesh are evident, which are: adultery, fornication, uncleanness, licentiousness, idolatry, sorcery, hatred, contentions, jealousies, outbursts of wrath, selfish ambitions, dissensions, heresies, envy, murders, drunkenness, revelries, and the like; of which I tell you beforehand, just as I also told you in time past, that those who practice such things will not inherit the kingdom of God.

—GALATIANS 5:19-21

For if anyone thinks himself to be something, when he is nothing, he deceives himself. But let each one examine his own work, and then he will have rejoicing in himself alone, and not in another. For each one shall bear his own load.

—GALATIANS 6:3-5

But let a man examine himself, and so let him eat of that bread and drink of that cup. For he who eats and drinks in an unworthy manner eats and drinks judgment to himself, not discerning the Lord's body. For this reason many are weak and sick among you, and many sleep. For if we would judge ourselves, we would not be judged. But when we are judged, we are chastened by the Lord, that we may not be condemned with the world.

—1 CORINTHIANS 11:28–32

■ Facing Secret Faults

Cleanse me from secret faults.
Keep back Your servant also from presumptuous sins;
Let them not have dominion over me.
Then I shall be blameless,
And I shall be innocent of great transgression.
Let the words of my mouth and the meditation of my heart
Be acceptable in Your sight,
O LORD, my strength and my redeemer.

—PSALM 19:12–14

For I know that in me (that is, in my flesh) nothing good dwells; for to will is present with me, but how to perform what is good I do not find. For the good that I will to do, I do not do; but the evil I will not to do, that I practice. Now if I do what I will not to do, it is no longer I who do it, but sin that dwells in me.

—ROMANS 7:18–20

■ *Accepting Correction*

He who keeps instruction is in the way of life,
But he who refuses reproof goes astray. . . .
He who despises the word will be destroyed,
But he who fears the commandment will be re-
warded.

—PROVERBS 10:17; 13:13

The backslider in heart will be filled with his
    own ways,
But a good man will be satisfied from above.

—PROVERBS 14:14

The ear that hears the reproof of life
Will abide among the wise.
He who disdains instruction despises his own
    soul,
But he who heeds reproof gets understanding.
The fear of the LORD is the instruction of
    wisdom,
And before honor is humility.

—PROVERBS 15:31–33

He who is often reproved, and hardens his
    neck,
Will suddenly be destroyed, and that without
    remedy. . . .
A man's pride will bring him low,
But the humble in spirit will retain honor.

—PROVERBS 29:1, 23

I Can't Deny It: I Have a God Who Cares

■ *God Uncovers All Things*

"Can anyone hide himself in secret places,
So I shall not see him?" says the LORD;
"Do I not fill heaven and earth?" says the LORD.
—JEREMIAH 23:24

Woe to those who seek deep to hide their
    counsel far from the LORD,
And their works are in the dark;
They say, "Who sees us?" and, "Who knows
    us?"
Surely you have things turned around!
Shall the potter be esteemed as the clay;
For shall the thing made say of him who made
    it,
"He did not make me"?
Or shall the thing formed say of him who
    formed it,
"He has no understanding"?
—ISAIAH 29:15–16

"Will it be well when [God] searches you out?
Or can you mock Him as one mocks a man?
He will surely reprove you
If you secretly show partiality.
Will not His excellence make you afraid,
And the dread of Him fall upon you? . . .
He also shall be my salvation,
For a hypocrite could not come before
    Him. . . .

Only two things do not do to me,
Then I will not hide myself from You:
Withdraw Your hand far from me,
And let not the dread of You make me afraid.
Then call, and I will answer;
Or let me speak, then You respond to me.
How many are my iniquities and sins?
Make me know my transgression and my sin."

—JOB 13:9–11, 16, 20–23

For the word of God is living and powerful, and sharper than any two-edged sword, piercing even to the division of soul and spirit, and of joints and marrow, and is a discerner of the thoughts and intents of the heart. And there is no creature hidden from His sight, but all things are naked and open to the eyes of Him to whom we must give account.

Seeing then that we have a great High Priest who has passed through the heavens, Jesus the Son of God, let us hold fast our confession. For we do not have a High Priest who cannot sympathize with our weaknesses, but was in all points tempted as we are, yet without sin. Let us therefore come boldly to the throne of grace, that we may obtain mercy and find grace to help in time of need.

—HEBREWS 4:12–16

■ God Knows Me Intimately

O LORD, You have searched me and known me.
You know my sitting down and my rising up;

You understand my thought afar off.
You comprehend my path and my lying down,
And are acquainted with all my ways.
For there is not a word on my tongue,
But behold, O LORD, You know it altogether.
You have hedged me behind and before,
And laid Your hand upon me.
Such knowledge is too wonderful for me;
It is high, I cannot attain it.
Where can I go from Your Spirit?
Or where can I flee from Your presence?
If I ascend into heaven, You are there;
If I make my bed in hell, behold, You are there.
If I take the wings of the morning,
And dwell in the uttermost parts of the sea,
Even there Your hand shall lead me,
And Your right hand shall hold me. . . .
Search me, O God, and know my heart;
Try me, and know my anxieties;
And see if there is any wicked way in me,
And lead me in the way everlasting.

—PSALM 139:1–10, 23–24

■ *God Calls for Repentance*

When I kept silent, my bones grew old
Through my groaning all the day long.
For day and night Your hand was heavy upon
me;
My vitality was turned into the drought of sum-
mer.
I acknowledged my sin to You,

And my iniquity I have not hidden.
I said, "I will confess my transgressions to the
LORD,"
And You forgave the iniquity of my sin.

—PSALM 32:3–5

"What man of you, having a hundred sheep, if
he loses one of them, does not leave the ninety-
nine in the wilderness, and go after the one which
is lost until he finds it? And when he has found it,
he lays it on his shoulders, rejoicing. And when he
comes home, he calls together his friends and
neighbors, saying to them, 'Rejoice with me, for I
have found my sheep which was lost!'

"I say to you that likewise there will be more joy
in heaven over one sinner who repents than over
ninety-nine just persons who need no repentance."

—LUKE 15:4–7

If we say that we have no sin, we deceive ourselves, and the truth is not in us. If we confess our
sins, He is faithful and just to forgive us our sins
and to cleanse us from all unrighteousness.

—1 JOHN 1:8–9

■ *God Offers Mercy*

He who covers his sins will not prosper,
But whoever confesses and forsakes them will
have mercy.

—PROVERBS 28:13

Do not withhold Your tender mercies from
   me, O LORD;
Let Your lovingkindness and Your truth
   continually preserve me.
For innumerable evils have surrounded me;
My iniquities have overtaken me, so that I am
   not able to look up;
They are more than the hairs of my head;
Therefore my heart fails me.
Be pleased, O LORD, to deliver me;
O LORD, make haste to help me!
                                        —PSALM 40:11–13

For I acknowledge my transgressions,
And my sin is ever before me.
Against You, You only, have I sinned,
And done this evil in Your sight—
That You may be found just when You speak,
And blameless when You judge.
                                        —PSALM 51:3–4

As a father pities his children,
So the LORD pities those who fear Him. . . .
But the mercy of the LORD is from everlasting
   to everlasting
On those who fear Him,
And His righteousness to children's children.
                                        —PSALM 103:13, 17

Therefore the LORD will wait, that He may be
   gracious to you;

And therefore He will be exalted, that He may
    have mercy on you.
For the LORD is a God of justice;
Blessed are all those who wait for Him.

—ISAIAH 30:18

For Those Worrying about What Can't Be Changed

Worry is a risky investment. It's placing a down payment on a future that may never come to pass. In fact, which one of your worries about a future scenario ever really turned out exactly as you envisioned it would, in all its glorious, projected devastation? It's impossible to imagine every possible consequence of every possible action that could take place before the expected disaster. Therefore, the situation could change completely in the very next instant.

So how much worry-energy is actually wasted energy? One hundred percent of it! Even if the situation does not change, our attitude toward it, our interpretation of it, can be radically transformed as soon as we wish it to be. We can simply ask ourselves as each event unfolds: What do I want this to mean? And we can choose to hear a gracious response: "God meant it for good, in order to bring it about as it is this day" (Gen. 50:20).

Restless? Worry Leads to Sleepless Nights

"Terrors are turned upon me;
They pursue my honor as the wind,
And my prosperity has passed like a cloud.
And now my soul is poured out because of
   my plight;
The days of affliction take hold of me.
My bones are pierced in me at night,
And my gnawing pains take no rest.
By great force my garment is disfigured;
It binds me about as the collar of my coat.
He has cast me into the mire,
And I have become like dust and ashes.
I cry out to You, but You do not answer me;
I stand up, and You regard me."

—JOB 30:15

My heart is in turmoil and cannot rest;
Days of affliction confront me.

—JOB 30:27

■ *Worrying about Daily Necessities?*

"Do not worry about your life, what you will eat or what you will drink; nor about your body, what you will put on. Is not life more than food and the body more than clothing?

"Look at the birds of the air, for they neither sow nor reap nor gather into barns; yet your heavenly Father feeds them. Are you not of more value than they?

"Which of you by worrying can add one cubit to his stature? So why do you worry about clothing? Consider the lilies of the field, how they grow: they neither toil nor spin; and yet I say to you that even Solomon in all his glory was not arrayed like one of these. Now if God so clothes the grass of the field, which today is, and tomorrow is thrown into the oven, will He not much more clothe you, O you of little faith?

"Therefore do not worry, saying, 'What shall we eat?' or 'What shall we drink?' or 'What shall we wear?' For after all these things the Gentiles seek. For your heavenly Father knows that you need all these things. But seek first the kingdom of God and His righteousness, and all these things shall be added to you."

—MATTHEW 6:25–33

■ *Worrying about Not Being Perfect?*

The pride of your heart has deceived you,
You who dwell in the clefts of the rock,
Whose habitation is high;
You who say in your heart,
"Who will bring me down to the ground?"

—OBADIAH 1:3

Only God is Perfect

He is the Rock, His work is perfect;
For all His ways are justice,
A God of truth and without injustice;
Righteous and upright is He.

—DEUTERONOMY 32:4

As for God, His way is perfect;
The word of the LORD is proven;
He is a shield to all who trust in Him.

—2 SAMUEL 22:31

Every good gift and every perfect gift is from above, and comes down from the Father of lights, with whom there is no variation or shadow of turning.

—JAMES 1:17

My Perfection Comes from God Alone

Now behold, one came and said to Him, "Good Teacher, what good thing shall I do that I may have eternal life?"

So He said to him, "Why do you call Me good? No one is good but One, that is, God. But if you want to enter into life, keep the commandments."

He said to Him, "Which ones?"

Jesus said, "'You shall not murder,' 'You shall not commit adultery,' 'You shall not steal,' 'You shall not bear false witness,' 'Honor your father and your mother,' and, 'You shall love your neighbor as yourself.'"

The young man said to Him, "All these things I have kept from my youth. What do I still lack?"

Jesus said to him, "If you want to be perfect, go, sell what you have and give to the poor, and you will have treasure in heaven; and come, follow Me."

But when the young man heard that saying, he went away sorrowful, for he had great possessions.

—MATTHEW 19:16–22

And He said to me, "My grace is sufficient for you, for My strength is made perfect in weakness." Therefore most gladly I will rather boast in my infirmities, that the power of Christ may rest upon me.

—2 CORINTHIANS 12:9

■ Worrying about Not Having Enough?

Then He called His twelve disciples together and gave them power and authority over all demons, and to cure diseases. He sent them to preach the kingdom of God and to heal the sick. And He said to them, "Take nothing for the journey, neither staffs nor bag nor bread nor money; and do not have two tunics apiece. Whatever house you enter, stay there, and from there depart."

—LUKE 9:1–4

Be anxious for nothing, but in everything by prayer and supplication, with thanksgiving, let your requests be made known to God; and the peace of God, which surpasses all understanding, will guard your hearts and minds through Christ Jesus.

—PHILIPPIANS 4:6–7

Not that I speak in regard to need, for I have learned in whatever state I am, to be content: I know how to be abased, and I know how to abound. Everywhere and in all things I have learned both to be full and to be hungry, both to abound and to suffer need. I can do all things through Christ who strengthens me.

—PHILIPPIANS 4:11–13

■ *Worrying about Money?*

"Do not lay up for yourselves treasures on earth, where moth and rust destroy and where thieves break in and steal; but lay up for yourselves treasures in heaven, where neither moth nor rust destroys and where thieves do not break in and steal. For where your treasure is, there your heart will be also.

"The lamp of the body is the eye. If therefore your eye is good, your whole body will be full of light. But if your eye is bad, your whole body will be full of darkness. If therefore the light that is in you is darkness, how great is that darkness!

"No one can serve two masters; for either he will hate the one and love the other, or else he will be loyal to the one and despise the other. You cannot serve God and mammon."

—MATTHEW 6:19–24

But godliness with contentment is great gain. For we brought nothing into this world, and it is certain we can carry nothing out. And having food and clothing, with these we shall be content. But those who desire to be rich fall into temptation and a snare, and into many foolish and harmful lusts which drown men in destruction and perdition. For the love of money is a root of all kinds of evil, for which some have strayed from the faith in their greediness, and pierced themselves through with many sorrows. But you, O man of God, flee these things and pursue righteousness, godliness, faith, love, patience, gentleness.

—1 TIMOTHY 6:6–11

■ Worrying about Personal Safety?

"And I say to you, My friends, do not be afraid of those who kill the body, and after that have no more that they can do. But I will show you whom you should fear: Fear Him who, after He has killed, has power to cast into hell; yes, I say to you, fear Him!

"Are not five sparrows sold for two copper coins? And not one of them is forgotten before God. But the very hairs of your head are all numbered. Do not fear therefore; you are of more value than many sparrows."

—LUKE 12:4-7

The LORD is my light and my salvation;
Whom shall I fear?
The LORD is the strength of my life;
Of whom shall I be afraid?
When the wicked came against me
To eat up my flesh,
My enemies and foes,
They stumbled and fell.
Though an army should encamp against me,
My heart shall not fear;
Though war should rise against me,
In this I will be confident.
One thing I have desired of the LORD,
That will I seek:
That I may dwell in the house of the LORD
All the days of my life,
To behold the beauty of the LORD,
And to inquire in His temple.
For in the time of trouble
He shall hide me in His pavilion;
In the secret place of His tabernacle
He shall hide me;
He shall set me high upon a rock. . . .
Wait on the LORD;
Be of good courage,
And He shall strengthen your heart;
Wait, I say, on the LORD!

—PSALM 27:1-5, 14

For God has not given us a spirit of fear, but of power and of love and of a sound mind.

—2 TIMOTHY 1:7

Therefore we will not fear,
Though the earth be removed,
And though the mountains be carried into the
  midst of the sea.

—PSALM 46:2

"Have I not commanded you? Be strong and of good courage; do not be afraid, nor be dismayed, for the LORD your God is with you wherever you go."

—JOSHUA 1:9

■ Worrying about Past Failure?

Now when they had kindled a fire in the midst of the courtyard and sat down together, Peter sat among them. And a certain servant girl, seeing him as he sat by the fire, looked intently at him and said, "This man was also with Him."

But he denied Him, saying, "Woman, I do not know Him."

And after a little while another saw him and said, "You also are of them."

But Peter said, "Man, I am not!"

Then after about an hour had passed, another confidently affirmed, saying, "Surely this fellow also was with Him, for he is a Galilean."

But Peter said, "Man, I do not know what you are saying!"

And immediately, while he was still speaking, the rooster crowed. And the Lord turned and looked at Peter. And Peter remembered the word of the Lord, how He had said to him, "Before the rooster crows, you will deny Me three times." Then Peter went out and wept bitterly.

—LUKE 22:55-62

Relax! Everything in God's Own Time

To everything there is a season,
A time for every purpose under heaven:
A time to be born,
And a time to die;
A time to plant,
And a time to pluck what is planted;
A time to kill,
And a time to heal;
A time to break down,
And a time to build up;
A time to weep,
And a time to laugh;
A time to mourn,
And a time to dance;
A time to cast away stones,
And a time to gather stones;
A time to embrace,
And a time to refrain from embracing;
A time to gain,

And a time to lose;
A time to keep,
And a time to throw away;
A time to tear,
And a time to sew;
A time to keep silence,
And a time to speak;
A time to love,
And a time to hate;
A time of war,
And a time of peace.

—ECCLESIASTES 3:1-8

■ God Gives Inner Peace

You will keep him in perfect peace,
Whose mind is stayed on You,
Because he trusts in You.

—ISAIAH 26:3

For he shall be like a tree planted by the
    waters,
Which spreads out its roots by the river,
And will not fear when heat comes;
But her leaf will be green,
And will not be anxious in the year of
    drought,
Nor will cease from yielding fruit.

—JEREMIAH 17:8

"Peace I leave with you, My peace I give to you;
not as the world gives do I give to you. Let not

your heart be troubled, neither let it be afraid."

—JOHN 14:27

"These things I have spoken to you, that in Me you may have peace. In the world you will have tribulation; but be of good cheer, I have overcome the world."

—JOHN 16:33

The peace of God, which surpasses all understanding, will guard your hearts and minds through Christ Jesus.

—PHILIPPIANS 4:7

Now may the Lord of peace Himself give you peace always in every way. The Lord be with you all.

—2 THESSALONIANS 3:16

■ *God Saves from Despair*

I will extol You, O LORD, for You have lifted
    me up,
And have not let my foes rejoice over me.
O LORD my God, I cried out to You,
And You have healed me.
O LORD, You brought my soul up from the
    grave;
You have kept me alive, that I should not go
    down to the pit.
Sing praise to the LORD, you saints of His,

And give thanks at the remembrance of His
   holy name.
For His anger is but for a moment,
His favor is for life;
Weeping may endure for a night,
But joy comes in the morning.

—PSALM 30:1–5

For the grace of God that brings salvation has
appeared to all men, teaching us that, denying ungodliness and worldly lusts, we should live soberly, righteously, and godly in the present age,
looking for the blessed hope and glorious appearing of our great God and Savior Jesus Christ, who
gave Himself for us, that He might redeem us
from every lawless deed and purify for Himself
His own special people, zealous for good works.

—TITUS 2:11–14

We are hard pressed on every side, yet not
crushed; we are perplexed, but not in despair;
persecuted, but not forsaken; struck down, but
not destroyed . . . knowing that He who raised up
the Lord Jesus will also raise us up with Jesus, and
will present us with you. . . . Therefore we do not
lose heart. Even though our outward man is perishing, yet the inward man is being renewed day
by day. For our light affliction, which is but for a
moment, is working for us a far more exceeding
and eternal weight of glory, while we do not look
at the things which are seen, but at the things

which are not seen. For the things which are seen
are temporary, but the things which are not seen
are eternal.

—2 CORINTHIANS 4:8–9, 14, 16–18

■ *God Replaces Fear and Worry with Joy*

Strengthen the weak hands,
And make firm the feeble knees.
Say to those who are fearful-hearted,
"Be strong, do not fear!
Behold, your God will come with vengeance,
With the recompense of God;
He will come and save you."
Then the eyes of the blind shall be opened,
And the ears of the deaf shall be unstopped.
Then the lame shall leap like a deer,
And the tongue of the dumb sing.
For waters shall burst forth in the wilderness,
And streams in the desert.
The parched ground shall become a pool,
And the thirsty land springs of water;
In the habitation of jackals, where each lay,
There shall be grass with reeds and rushes.
A highway shall be there, and a road,
And it shall be called the Highway of
    Holiness.
The unclean shall not pass over it,
But it shall be for others.
Whoever walks the road, although a fool,
Shall not go astray.
No lion shall be there,

Nor shall any ravenous beast go up on it;
It shall not be found there.
But the redeemed shall walk there,
And the ransomed of the LORD shall return,
And come to Zion with singing,
With everlasting joy on their heads.
They shall obtain joy and gladness,
And sorrow and sighing shall flee away.

—ISAIAH 35:3-10

■ *God Provides the Ultimate Future Security*

If in this life only we have hope in Christ, we are of all men the most pitiable. But now Christ is risen from the dead, and has become the firstfruits of those who have fallen asleep. . . .

Behold, I tell you a mystery: We shall not all sleep, but we shall all be changed—in a moment, in the twinkling of an eye, at the last trumpet. For the trumpet will sound, and the dead will be raised incorruptible, and we shall be changed. For this corruptible must put on incorruption, and this mortal must put on immortality. So when this corruptible has put on incorruption, and this mortal has put on immortality, then shall be brought to pass the saying that is written: "Death is swallowed up in victory."

"O Death, where is your sting?
O Hades, where is your victory?"

—1 CORINTHIANS 15:19-20, 51-55

For Those Worrying about What Can't Be Changed 113

But I do not want you to be ignorant, brethren, concerning those who have fallen asleep, lest you sorrow as others who have no hope. For if we believe that Jesus died and rose again, even so God will bring with Him those who sleep in Jesus. For this we say to you by the word of the Lord, that we who are alive and remain until the coming of the Lord will by no means precede those who are asleep. For the Lord Himself will descend from heaven with a shout, with the voice of an archangel, and with the trumpet of God. And the dead in Christ will rise first.

Then we who are alive and remain shall be caught up together with them in the clouds to meet the Lord in the air. And thus we shall always be with the Lord. Therefore comfort one another with these words.

—1 THESSALONIANS 4:13–18

For Those Living by Extremes

Robert was a thirty-five-year-old minister who usually kept himself under tight control. Yet every once in a while, Robert would sneak pornography into his home. His intense control seemed to burst its boundaries at those times and flow into unbridled lust. He knew it was wrong, but he almost felt compelled to do something, sometimes, to offset the strict, unbending rules he had set down for every part of his life. He would feel out of control until he repented, felt he had atoned for his sins, and replaced his armorlike appearance "togetherness."

Have you ever known someone who needed to be in crisis? They are the people living by extremes: from full control to no control; from strict discipline to lazy apathy; from creative paralysis to extreme overwork; from torrid rage to apparent kindness; from deep faith, to no faith.

The "cure" for living by extremes is pretty

plain and unspectacular: basic accountability, obedience, endurance, patience, discipline, etc. But as you read the Scriptures dealing with those topics, be sure to envision yourself enfolded by the mighty GRACE of God, without which no mere human attempt at personal transformation could ever be possible.

Accountability

■ . . . To My Authorities

Let every soul be subject to the governing authorities. For there is no authority except from God, and the authorities that exist are appointed by God. Therefore whoever resists the authority resists the ordinance of God, and those who resist will bring judgment on themselves. For rulers are not a terror to good works, but to evil.

Do you want to be unafraid of the authority? Do what is good, and you will have praise from the same. For he is God's minister to you for good. But if you do evil, be afraid; for he does not bear the sword in vain; for he is God's minister, an avenger to execute wrath on him who practices evil.

Therefore you must be subject, not only because of wrath but also for conscience' sake. For because of this you also pay taxes, for they are God's ministers attending continually to this very thing. Render therefore to all their due: taxes to whom taxes are due, customs to whom customs, fear to whom fear, honor to whom honor. Owe no one anything except to love one another, for he who loves another has fulfilled the law. . . .

Let us walk properly, as in the day, not in revelry and drunkenness, not in licentiousness and lewdness, not in strife and envy. But put on the Lord Jesus Christ, and make no provision for the flesh, to fulfill its lusts.

—ROMANS 13:1–8, 13–14

■ . . . *To My Neighbor*

"And who is my neighbor?"

Then Jesus answered and said: "A certain man went down from Jerusalem to Jericho, and fell among thieves, who stripped him of his clothing, wounded him, and departed, leaving him half dead.

"Now by chance a certain priest came down that road. And when he saw him, he passed by on the other side. Likewise a Levite, when he arrived at the place, came and looked, and passed by on the other side. But a certain Samaritan, as he journeyed, came where he was. And when he saw him, he had compassion on him, and went to him and bandaged his wounds, pouring on oil and wine; and he set him on his own animal, brought him to an inn, and took care of him.

"On the next day, when he departed, he took out two denarii, gave them to the innkeeper, and said to him, 'Take care of him; and whatever more you spend, when I come again, I will repay you.'

"So which of these three do you think was neighbor to him who fell among the thieves?"

And he said, "He who showed mercy on him."

Then Jesus said to him, "Go and do likewise."

—LUKE 10:29–37

■ . . . *In My Choice of Friends*

Blessed is the man
Who walks not in the counsel of the ungodly,
Nor stands in the path of sinners,
Nor sits in the seat of the scornful;
But his delight is in the law of the LORD,
And in His law he meditates day and night.
He shall be like a tree
Planted by the rivers of water,
That brings forth its fruit in its season,
Whose leaf also shall not wither;
And whatever he does shall prosper.
The ungodly are not so,
But are like the chaff which the wind drives away.
Therefore the ungodly shall not stand in the judgment,
Nor sinners in the congregation of the righteous.
For the LORD knows the way of the righteous,
But the way of the ungodly shall perish.

—PSALM 1:1–6

■ . . . In My Responsibilities

Do not love sleep, lest you come to poverty;
Open your eyes, and you will be satisfied
   with bread.

—PROVERBS 20:13

I went by the field of the slothful,
And by the vineyard of the man devoid of
   understanding;
And there it was, all overgrown with thorns;
Its surface was covered with nettles;
Its stone wall was broken down.
When I saw it, I considered it well;
I looked on it and received instruction:
A little sleep, a little slumber,
A little folding of the hands to rest;
So your poverty will come like a prowler,
And your want like an armed man.

—PROVERBS 24:30-34

Aspire to lead a quiet life, to mind your own business, and to work with your own hands, as we commanded you, that you may walk properly toward those who are outside, and that you may lack nothing.

—1 THESSALONIANS 4:11b-12

For even when we were with you, we commanded you this: If anyone will not work, neither shall he eat. For we hear that there are some who walk among you in a disorderly manner, not working at all, but are busybodies. Now those who are such we command and exhort through our Lord Jesus Christ that they work in quietness and eat their own bread.

—2 THESSALONIANS 3:10–12

■ . . . *With My Sexuality*

For this is the will of God, your sanctification: that you should abstain from sexual immorality; that each of you should know how to possess his own vessel in sanctification and honor, not in passion of lust, like the Gentiles who do not know God; that no one should take advantage of and defraud his brother in this matter, because the Lord is the avenger of all such, as we also forewarned you and testified. For God did not call us to uncleanness, but in holiness. Therefore he who rejects this does not reject man, but God, who has also given us His Holy Spirit.

—1 THESSALONIANS 4:3–8

But fornication and all uncleanness or covetousness, let it not even be named among you, as is fitting for saints; neither filthiness, nor foolish talking, nor coarse jesting, which are not fitting, but rather giving of thanks. For this you know, that no fornicator, unclean person, nor covetous man, who is an idolater, has any inheritance in the kingdom of Christ and God. Let no one deceive you with empty words, for because of these things the wrath of God comes upon the sons of disobedience. Therefore do not be partakers with them. . . . And do not be drunk with wine, in which is dissipation; but be filled with the Spirit.

—EPHESIANS 5:3–7, 18

■ . . . *With My Moodiness and Anger*

Be angry, and do not sin.
Meditate within your heart on your bed, and
  be still.

—PSALM 4:4

"But I say to you that whoever is angry with his brother without a cause shall be in danger of the judgment. And whoever says to his brother, 'Raca!' shall be in danger of the council. But whoever says, 'You fool!' shall be in danger of hell fire."

—MATTHEW 5:22

"Be angry, and do not sin": do not let the sun go down on your wrath.

—EPHESIANS 4:26

Obedience

"Not everyone who says to Me, 'Lord, Lord,' shall enter the kingdom of heaven, but he who does the will of My Father in heaven. Many will say to Me in that day, 'Lord, Lord, have we not prophesied in Your name, cast out demons in Your name, and done many wonders in Your name?' And then I will declare to them, 'I never knew you; depart from Me, you who practice lawlessness!'

"Therefore whoever hears these sayings of Mine, and does them, I will liken him to a wise man who built his house on the rock: and the rain descended, the floods came, and the winds blew and beat on that house; and it did not fall, for it was founded on the rock. Now everyone who hears these sayings of Mine, and does not do them, will be like a foolish man who built his house on the sand: and the rain descended, the floods came, and the winds blew and beat on that house; and it fell. And great was its fall."

—MATTHEW 7:21–27

But be doers of the word, and not hearers only, deceiving yourselves. For if anyone is a hearer of the word and not a doer, he is like a man observing his natural face in a mirror; for he observes himself, goes away, and immediately forgets what kind of man he was. But he who looks into the perfect law of liberty and continues in it, and is not a forgetful hearer but a doer of the work, this one will be blessed in what he does.

If anyone among you thinks he is religious, and does not bridle his tongue but deceives his own heart, this one's religion is useless. Pure and undefiled religion before God and the Father is this:

to visit orphans and widows in their trouble, and to keep oneself unspotted from the world.

—JAMES 1:22–27

Endurance

"Tell us, when will these things be? And what will be the sign when all these things will be fulfilled?"

And Jesus, answering them, began to say: "Take heed that no one deceives you. For many will come in My name, saying, 'I am He,' and will deceive many.

"But when you hear of wars and rumors of wars, do not be troubled; for such things must happen, but the end is not yet. For nation will rise against nation, and kingdom against kingdom. And there will be earthquakes in various places, and there will be famines and troubles. These are the beginnings of sorrows.

"But watch out for yourselves, for they will deliver you up to councils, and you will be beaten in the synagogues. And you will be brought before rulers and kings for My sake, for a testimony to them. And the gospel must first be preached to all the nations. But when they arrest you and deliver you up, do not worry beforehand, or premeditate what you will speak. But whatever is given you in that hour, speak that; for it is not you who speak, but the Holy Spirit.

"Now brother will betray brother to death, and a father his child; and children will rise up against parents and cause them to be put to death. And you will be hated by all for My name's sake. But he who endures to the end shall be saved."

—MARK 13:4–13

You therefore must endure hardship as a good soldier of Jesus Christ.

—2 TIMOTHY 2:3

If we endure,
We shall also reign with Him.
If we deny Him,
He also will deny us.

—2 TIMOTHY 2:12

But you have carefully followed my doctrine, manner of life, purpose, faith, longsuffering, love, perseverance.

—2 TIMOTHY 3:10

But you be watchful in all things, endure afflictions, do the work of an evangelist, fulfill your ministry.

—2 TIMOTHY 4:5

Therefore we also, since we are surrounded by so great a cloud of witnesses, let us lay aside every weight, and the sin which so easily ensnares us, and let us run with endurance the race that is set before us, looking unto Jesus, the author and finisher of our faith, who for the joy that was set before Him endured the cross, despising the shame, and has sat down at the right hand of the throne of God. For consider Him who endured such hostility from sinners against Himself, lest you become weary and discouraged in your souls. You have not yet resisted to bloodshed, striving against sin. . . . Therefore strengthen the hands which hang down, and the feeble knees, and make straight paths for your feet, so that what is lame may not be dislocated, but rather be healed.

—HEBREWS 12:1–4, 12–13

Perseverance

Therefore, having been justified by faith, we have peace with God through our Lord Jesus Christ, through whom also we have access by faith into this grace in which we stand, and rejoice in hope of the glory of God. And not only that, but we also glory in tribulations, knowing that tribulation produces perseverance; and perseverance, character; and character, hope.

—ROMANS 5:1–4

For we know that the whole creation groans and labors with birth pangs together until now. And not only they, but we also who have the firstfruits of the Spirit, even we ourselves groan within ourselves, eagerly waiting for the adoption, the redemption of our body. For we were saved in this hope, but hope that is seen is not hope; for why does one still hope for what he sees? But if we hope for what we do not see, then we eagerly wait for it with perseverance.

—ROMANS 8:22-25

Patience

My brethren, count it all joy when you fall into various trials, knowing that the testing of your faith produces patience. But let patience have its perfect work, that you may be perfect and complete, lacking nothing. If any of you lacks wisdom, let him ask of God, who gives to all liberally and without reproach, and it will be given to him. But let him ask in faith, with no doubting, for he who doubts is like a wave of the sea driven and tossed by the wind. For let not that man suppose that he will receive anything from the Lord; he is a double-minded man, unstable in all his ways.

—JAMES 1:2-8

Discipline

Do you not know that those who run in a race all run, but one receives the prize? Run in such a way that you may obtain it. And everyone who competes for the prize is temperate in all things. Now they do it to obtain a perishable crown, but we for an imperishable crown. Therefore I run thus: not with uncertainty. Thus I fight: not as one who beats the air. But I discipline my body and bring it into subjection, lest, when I have preached to others, I myself should become disqualified.

—1 CORINTHIANS 9:24–27

I charge you therefore before God and the Lord Jesus Christ, who will judge the living and the dead at His appearing and His kingdom: Preach the word! Be ready in season and out of season. Convince, rebuke, exhort, with all longsuffering and teaching. For the time will come when they will not endure sound doctrine, but according to their own desires, because they have itching ears, they will heap up for themselves teachers; and they will turn their ears away from the truth, and be turned aside to fables.

But you be watchful in all things, endure afflictions, do the work of an evangelist, fulfill your ministry. For I am already being poured out as a drink offering, and the time of my departure is at hand. I have fought the good fight, I have finished the race, I have kept the faith.

—2 TIMOTHY 4:1–7

CHAPTER 10

For Those Looking for What Is Lacking in Life

Something is missing! It has been said that we have a God-shaped vacuum built into us, and that our souls are restless until that big empty place is filled up with Him. What do you do with your own empty place? The place may very well be God-shaped, but it was formed not only by God but by every experience you had that fell short of God's unconditional love and care for you—namely, every experience of human inability to fully satisfy your needs for love and approval. That's a big empty space where childhood nurture and messages of worth are missing.

Now, as adults, we look around for meaning and purpose in life, usually feeling restless and discontented. We can't seem to get comfortable just being with "me." We look for things to place in the God-shaped vacuum, and some of them seem to fit for a while. But each of those hope-encased finite solutions, offered to an infinite need, ultimately fails to fill the void; once again we're restless.

Looking for What's Missing

Out of the depths I have cried to You, O
 LORD;
Lord, hear my voice!
Let Your ears be attentive
To the voice of my supplications.
If You, LORD, should mark iniquities,
O Lord, who could stand?
But there is forgiveness with You,
That You many be feared.
I wait for the LORD, my soul waits,
And in His word I do hope.
My soul waits for the Lord
More than those who watch for the morning—
I say, more than those who watch for the
 morning.

—PSALM 130:1–6

I cry out to the LORD with my voice;
With my voice to the LORD I make my
 supplication.
I pour out my complaint before Him;
I declare before Him my trouble.
When my spirit was overwhelmed within me,
Then You knew my path.
In the way in which I walk

They have secretly set a snare for me.
Look on my right hand and see,
For there is no one who acknowledges me;
Refuge has failed me;
No one cares for my soul.
I cried out to You, O LORD:
I said, "You are my refuge,
My portion in the land of the living.
Attend to my cry,
For I am brought very low;
Deliver me from my persecutors,
For they are stronger than I."

—PSALM 142:1–6

Understanding God's Offer of a Better Way

■ *God Chooses Us*

He chose us in Him before the foundation of the
world, that we should be holy and without blame
before Him in love, having predestined us to
adoption as sons by Jesus Christ to Himself, according to the good pleasure of His will, to the
praise of the glory of His grace, by which He has
made us accepted in the Beloved.

In Him we have redemption through His blood,
the forgiveness of sins, according to the riches of
His grace which He made to abound toward us in
all wisdom and prudence, having made known to
us the mystery of His will, according to His good
pleasure which He purposed in Himself, that in

the dispensation of the fullness of the times He might gather together in one all things in Christ, both which are in heaven and which are on earth—in Him, in whom also we have obtained an inheritance, being predestined according to the purpose of Him who works all things according to the counsel of His will, that we who first trusted in Christ should be to the praise of His glory. In Him you also trusted, after you heard the word of truth, the gospel of your salvation; in whom also, having believed, you were sealed with the Holy Spirit of promise, who is the guarantee of our inheritance until the redemption of the purchased possession, to the praise of His glory.

—EPHESIANS 1:4b–14

■ *Christ Calls Us*

"Come to Me, all you who labor and are heavy laden, and I will give you rest. Take My yoke upon you and learn from Me, for I am gentle and lowly in heart, and you will find rest for your souls. For My yoke is easy and My burden is light."

—MATTHEW 11:28–30

On the last day, that great day of the feast, Jesus stood and cried out, saying, "If anyone thirsts, let him come to Me and drink. He who believes in Me, as the Scripture has said, out of his heart will flow rivers of living water."

—JOHN 7:37–38

■ Grace Saves Us

For by grace you have been saved through faith, and that not of yourselves; it is the gift of God, not of works, lest anyone should boast.

—EPHESIANS 2:8–9

But now the righteousness of God apart from the law is revealed, being witnessed by the Law and the Prophets, even the righteousness of God which is through faith in Jesus Christ to all and on all who believe. For there is no difference; for all have sinned and fall short of the glory of God, being justified freely by His grace through the redemption that is in Christ Jesus.

—ROMANS 3:21–24

Therefore, having been justified by faith, we have peace with God through our Lord Jesus Christ. . . . But God demonstrates His own love toward us, in that while we were still sinners, Christ died for us. Much more then, having now been justified by His blood, we shall be saved from wrath through Him. For if when we were enemies we were reconciled to God through the death of His Son, much more, having been reconciled, we shall be saved by His life. And not only that, but we also rejoice in God through our Lord Jesus Christ, through whom we have now received the reconciliation.

—ROMANS 5:1, 8–11

■ Belief Brings Us Righteousness

If you confess with your mouth the Lord Jesus and believe in your heart that God has raised Him from the dead, you will be saved. For with the heart one believes to righteousness, and with the mouth confession is made to salvation. For the Scripture says, "Whoever believes on Him will not be put to shame." For there is no distinction between Jew and Greek, for the same Lord over all is rich to all who call upon Him. For "whoever calls on the name of the LORD shall be saved."

—ROMANS 10:9–13

Filling the Soul-Vacuum with God

Bless the LORD, O my soul,
And forget not all His benefits:
Who forgives all your iniquities,
Who heals all your diseases,
Who redeems your life from destruction,
Who crowns you with lovingkindness and
     tender mercies,
Who satisfies your mouth with good things,
So that your youth is renewed like the eagle's.
—PSALM 103:2–5

The poor shall eat and be satisfied;
Those who seek Him will praise the LORD.
Let your heart live forever! . . .

All the prosperous of the earth
Shall eat and worship;
All those who go down to the dust
Shall bow before Him,
Even he who cannot keep himself alive.
—PSALM 22:26, 29

"Come, eat of my bread
And drink of the wine I have mixed."
—PROVERBS 9:5

"Ho! Everyone who thirsts,
Come to the waters;
And you who have no money,
Come, buy and eat.
Yes, come, buy wine and milk
Without money and without price.
Why do you spend money for what is not
  bread,
And your wages for what does not satisfy?
Listen diligently to Me, and eat what is good,
And let your soul delight itself in abundance."
—ISAIAH 55:1–2

You shall eat in plenty and be satisfied,
And praise the name of the LORD your God,
Who has dealt wondrously with you;
And My people shall never be put to shame.
—JOEL 2:26

Now when one of those who sat at the table with
Him heard these things, he said to Him, "Blessed

is he who shall eat bread in the kingdom of God!"

—LUKE 14:15

For this reason I bow my knees to the Father of our Lord Jesus Christ, from whom the whole family in heaven and earth is named, that He would grant you, according to the riches of His glory, to be strengthened with might through His Spirit in the inner man, that Christ may dwell in your hearts through faith; that you, being rooted and grounded in love, may be able to comprehend with all the saints what is the width and length and depth and height—to know the love of Christ which passes knowledge; that you may be filled with all the fullness of God.

—EPHESIANS 3:14–19

■ *Scripture Reading*

Blessed are the undefiled in the way,
Who walk in the law of the LORD!
Blessed are those who keep His testimonies,
Who seek Him with the whole heart!
They also do no iniquity;
They walk in His ways.
You have commanded us
To keep Your precepts diligently.
Oh, that my ways were directed
To keep Your statutes!
Then I would not be ashamed,
When I look into all Your commandments.
I will praise You with uprightness of heart,

When I learn Your righteous judgments.
I will keep Your statutes;
Oh, do not forsake me utterly!
How can a young man cleanse his way?
By taking heed according to Your word.
With my whole heart I have sought You;
Oh, let me not wander from Your
    commandments!
Your word I have hidden in my heart,
That I might not sin against You.
Blessed are You, O LORD!
Teach me Your statutes!
With my lips I have declared
All the judgments of Your mouth.
I have rejoiced in the way of Your testimonies,
As much as in all riches.
I will meditate on Your precepts,
And contemplate Your ways.
I will delight myself in Your statutes;
I will not forget Your word.

—PSALM 119:1–16

■ Prayer

Pray without ceasing, in everything give thanks; for this is the will of God in Christ Jesus for you. Do not quench the Spirit. Do not despise prophecies. Test all things; hold fast what is good. Abstain from every form of evil.

—1 THESSALONIANS 5:17–22

Is anyone among you suffering? Let him pray. Is anyone cheerful? Let him sing psalms. Is anyone among you sick? Let him call for the elders of the church, and let them pray over him, anointing him with oil in the name of the Lord. And the prayer of faith will save the sick, and the Lord will raise him up. And if he has committed sins, he will be forgiven. Confess your trespasses to one another, and pray for one another, that you may be healed.

The effective, fervent prayer of a righteous man avails much. Elijah was a man with a nature like ours, and he prayed earnestly that it would not rain; and it did not rain on the land for three years and six months. And he prayed again, and the heaven gave rain, and the earth produced its fruit.

—JAMES 5:13–18

■ *Worship*

Oh, give thanks to the LORD!
Call upon His name;
Make known His deeds among the peoples.
Sing to Him, sing psalms to Him;
Talk of all His wondrous works.
Glory in His holy name;
Let the hearts of those rejoice who seek the
    LORD.
Seek the LORD and His strength;
Seek His face evermore.

—PSALM 105:1–4

Jesus said to her, "Woman, believe Me, the hour is coming when you will neither on this mountain, nor in Jerusalem, worship the Father. You worship what you do not know; we know what we worship, for salvation is of the Jews.

"But the hour is coming, and now is, when the true worshipers will worship the Father in spirit and truth; for the Father is seeking such to worship Him. God is Spirit, and those who worship Him must worship in spirit and truth."

—JOHN 4:21–24

The twenty-four elders fall down before Him who sits on the throne and worship Him who lives forever and ever, and cast their crowns before the throne.

—REVELATION 4:10

"Fear God and give glory to Him, for the hour of His judgment has come; and worship Him who made heaven and earth, the sea and springs of water."

—REVELATION 14:7

"Who shall not fear You, O Lord, and glorify
   Your name?
For You alone are holy.
For all nations shall come and worship before
   You,
For Your judgments have been manifested."

—REVELATION 15:4

■ *Good Works*

But be doers of the word, and not hearers only, deceiving yourselves. For if anyone is a hearer of the word and not a doer, he is like a man observing his natural face in a mirror; for he observes himself, goes away, and immediately forgets what kind of man he was. But he who looks into the perfect law of liberty and continues in it, and is not a forgetful hearer but a doer of the work, this one will be blessed in what he does. . . . Pure and undefiled religion before God and the Father is this: to visit orphans and widows in their trouble, and to keep oneself unspotted from the world.

—JAMES 1:22–25, 27

■ *Commitment*

For to me, to live is Christ, and to die is gain.
—PHILIPPIANS 1:21

But what things were gain to me, these I have counted loss for Christ. But indeed I also count all things loss for the excellence of the knowledge of Christ Jesus my Lord, for whom I have suffered the loss of all things, and count them as rubbish, that I may gain Christ and be found in Him, not having my own righteousness, which is from the law, but that which is through faith in Christ, the righteousness which is from God by faith; that I may know Him and the power of His resurrection, and the fellowship of His sufferings, being conformed to His death, if, by any means, I may attain to the resurrection from the dead. Not that I have already attained, or am already perfected; but I press on, that I may lay hold of that for which Christ Jesus has also laid hold of me. Brethren, I do not count myself to have apprehended; but one thing I do, forgetting those things which are behind and reaching forward to those things which are ahead, I press toward the goal for the prize of the upward call of God in Christ Jesus.

—PHILIPPIANS 3:7–14

As you have therefore received Christ Jesus the Lord, so walk in Him, rooted and built up in Him and established in the faith, as you have been taught, abounding in it with thanksgiving. Beware lest anyone cheat you through philosophy and empty deceit, according to the tradition of men, according to the basic principles of the world, and not according to Christ. For in Him dwells all the fullness of the Godhead bodily; and you are complete in Him, who is the head of all principality and power.

—COLOSSIANS 2:6–10

■ Inner Peace

You will keep him in perfect peace,
Whose mind is stayed on You,
Because he trusts in You.

—ISAIAH 26:3

For he shall be like a tree planted by the
   waters, Which spreads out its roots by the
   river,
And will not fear when heat comes;
But her leaf will be green,
And will not be anxious in the year of
   drought,
Nor will cease from yielding fruit.

—JEREMIAH 17:8

"Peace I leave with you, My peace I give to you;
not as the world gives do I give to you. Let not
your heart be troubled, neither let it be afraid."

—JOHN 14:27

"These things I have spoken to you, that in Me
you may have peace. In the world you will have
tribulation; but be of good cheer, I have overcome
the world."

—JOHN 16:33

For God is not the author of confusion but of
peace, as in all the churches of the saints.

—1 CORINTHIANS 14:33

For He Himself is our peace, who has made
both one, and has broken down the middle wall of
division between us, having abolished in His flesh
the enmity, that is, the law of commandments con-
tained in ordinances, so as to create in Himself one
new man from the two, thus making peace. . . .

And He came and preached peace to you who were afar off and to those who were near.

—EPHESIANS 2:14–15, 17

The peace of God, which surpasses all understanding, will guard your hearts and minds through Christ Jesus.

—PHILIPPIANS 4:7

Now may the Lord of peace Himself give you peace always in every way. The Lord be with you all.

—2 THESSALONIANS 3:16

Carrying the Recovery Message to Others

Jesus said it to a man He had just healed: Go home and tell about God's goodness to you.

What about you? Have you experienced some healing? How did it happen? Was it all your doing? Or can you give a word of recommendation to your Higher Power?

"You can't keep it unless you give it away." The ultimate paradox! Yet we know it's true. Ultimately, we want happiness. But we know it will only come when we release our white-knuckled grasp on what we think will get it for us (name your addiction here: _____) and turn our attention to making the lives of others a little more happy.

Thanking God for My Own 'Spiritual Awakening'

It is good to give thanks to the LORD,
And to sing praises to Your name, O Most
   High;
To declare Your lovingkindness in the
   morning,
And Your faithfulness every night,
On an instrument of ten strings,
On the lute,
And on the harp,
With harmonious sound.
For You, LORD, have made me glad through
   Your work;
I will triumph in the works of Your hands.

                       —PSALM 92:1–4

Oh, sing to the LORD a new song!
Sing to the LORD, all the earth.
Sing to the LORD, bless His name;
Proclaim the good news of His salvation from
   day to day.

                       —PSALM 96:1–2

Praise the LORD!
Oh, give thanks to the LORD, for He is good!
For His mercy endures forever.
Who can utter the mighty acts of the LORD?
Or can declare all His praise?
Blessed are those who keep justice,

And he who does righteousness at all times!
—PSALM 106:1-3

Oh, give thanks to the LORD, for He is good!
For His mercy endures forever.
Let the redeemed of the LORD say so,
Whom He has redeemed from the hand of the
  enemy.

—PSALM 107:1-2

Oh, that men would give thanks to the LORD
  for His goodness,
And for His wonderful works to the children
  of men!
Let them sacrifice the sacrifices of
  thanksgiving,
And declare His works with rejoicing.
—PSALM 107:21-22

Praise the LORD!
I will praise the LORD with my whole heart,
In the assembly of the upright and in the
  congregation.
The works of the LORD are great,
Studied by all who have pleasure in them.
His work is honorable and glorious,
And His righteousness endures forever.
He has made His wonderful works to be
  remembered;
The LORD is gracious and full of compassion.
He has given food to those who fear Him;

He will ever be mindful of His covenant.
He has declared to His people the power of
    His works,
In giving them the heritage of the nations.
The works of His hands are verity and justice;
All His precepts are sure.
They stand fast forever and ever,
And are done in truth and uprightness.
He has sent redemption to His people;
He has commanded His covenant forever:
Holy and awesome is His name.
The fear of the LORD is the beginning of
    wisdom;
A good understanding have all those who do
    His commandments.
His praise endures forever.

—PSALM 111:1–10

I will extol You, my God, O King;
And I will bless Your name forever and ever.
Every day I will bless You,
And I will praise Your name forever and ever.
Great is the LORD, and greatly to be praised;
And His greatness is unsearchable.
One generation shall praise Your works to
    another,
And shall declare Your mighty acts.
I will meditate on the glorious splendor of
    Your majesty,
And on Your wondrous works.
Men shall speak of the might of Your awesome
    acts,

And I will declare Your greatness.
They shall utter the memory of Your great
    goodness,
And shall sing of Your righteousness.
The LORD is gracious and full of compassion,
Slow to anger and great in mercy.
The LORD is good to all,
And His tender mercies are over all His
    works.
All Your works shall praise You, O LORD,
And Your saints shall bless You.
They shall speak of the glory of Your
    kingdom,
And talk of Your power,
To make known to the sons of men His
    mighty acts, And the glorious majesty of
    His kingdom. . . .
My mouth shall speak the praise of the LORD,
And all flesh shall bless His holy name
Forever and ever.

—PSALM 145:1–12, 21

And I thank Christ Jesus our Lord who has en-
abled me, because He counted me faithful, putting me into the ministry, although I was formerly
a blasphemer, a persecutor, and an insolent man;
but I obtained mercy because I did it ignorantly in
unbelief. And the grace of our Lord was exceedingly abundant, with faith and love which are in
Christ Jesus. This is a faithful saying and worthy
of all acceptance, that Christ Jesus came into the
world to save sinners, of whom I am chief. How-

ever, for this reason I obtained mercy, that in me first Jesus Christ might show all longsuffering, as a pattern to those who are going to believe on Him for everlasting life.

—1 TIMOTHY 1:12–16

Befriending Those Looking for What's Missing

Out of the depths I have cried to You, O
    LORD;
Lord, hear my voice!
Let Your ears be attentive
To the voice of my supplications.
If You, LORD, should mark iniquities,
O Lord, who could stand?
But there is forgiveness with You,
That You may be feared.
I wait for the LORD, my soul waits,
And in His word I do hope.
My soul waits for the Lord
More than those who watch for the morning—
I say, more than those who watch for the
    morning.

—PSALM 130:1–6

I cry out to the LORD with my voice;
With my voice to the LORD I make my
    supplication.
I pour out my complaint before Him;
I declare before Him my trouble.
When my spirit was overwhelmed within me,

Then You knew my path.
In the way in which I walk
They have secretly set a snare for me.
Look on my right hand and see,
For there is no one who acknowledges me;
Refuge has failed me;
No one cares for my soul.

—PSALM 142:1–4

■ *God Can Fill Their Emptiness*

Come to Me, all you who labor and are heavy laden, and I will give you rest. Take My yoke upon you and learn from Me, for I am gentle and lowly in heart, and you will find rest for your souls. For My yoke is easy and My burden is light.

—MATTHEW 11:28–30

On the last day, that great day of the feast, Jesus stood and cried out, saying, "If anyone thirsts, let him come to Me and drink. He who believes in Me, as the Scripture has said, out of his heart will flow rivers of living water."

—JOHN 7:37–38

Bless the LORD, O my soul,
And forget not all His benefits:
Who forgives all your iniquities,
Who heals all your diseases,
Who redeems your life from destruction,
Who crowns you with lovingkindness and
    tender mercies,

Who satisfies your mouth with good things,
So that your youth is renewed like the eagle's.
—PSALM 103:2-5

The poor shall eat and be satisfied;
Those who seek Him will praise the LORD.
Let your heart live forever! . . .
All the prosperous of the earth
Shall eat and worship;
All those who go down to the dust
Shall bow before Him,
Even he who cannot keep himself alive.
—PSALM 22:26, 29

"Come, eat of my bread
And drink of the wine I have mixed."
—PROVERBS 9:5

"Ho! Everyone who thirsts,
Come to the waters;
And you who have no money,
Come, buy and eat.
Yes, come, buy wine and milk
Without money and without price.
Why do you spend money for what is not
    bread,
And your wages for what does not satisfy?
Listen diligently to Me, and eat what is good,
And let your soul delight itself in abundance."
—ISAIAH 55:1-2

"You shall eat in plenty and be satisfied,
And praise the name of the LORD your God,
Who has dealt wondrously with you;
And My people shall never be put to shame."

—JOEL 2:26

Now when one of those who sat at the table with Him heard these things, he said to Him, "Blessed is he who shall eat bread in the kingdom of God!"

—LUKE 14:15

For this reason I bow my knees to the Father of our Lord Jesus Christ, from whom the whole family in heaven and earth is named, that He would grant you, according to the riches of His glory, to be strengthened with might through His Spirit in the inner man, that Christ may dwell in your hearts through faith; that you, being rooted and grounded in love, may be able to comprehend with all the saints what is the width and length and depth and height—to know the love of Christ which passes knowledge; that you may be filled with all the fullness of God.

—EPHESIANS 3:14–19

■ *God Can Give Them the Benefits of Belief Too*

But as many as received Him, to them He gave the right to become children of God, even to those who believe in His name: who were born, not of blood, nor of the will of the flesh, nor of the will of man, but of God.

—JOHN 1:12–13

"Most assuredly, I say to you, he who hears My word and believes in Him who sent Me has everlasting life, and shall not come into judgment, but has passed from death into life."

—JOHN 5:24

There is therefore now no condemnation to those who are in Christ Jesus, who do not walk according to the flesh, but according to the Spirit.

—ROMANS 8:1

Blessed be the God and Father of our Lord Jesus Christ, who according to His abundant mercy has begotten us again to a living hope through the resurrection of Jesus Christ from the dead, to an inheritance incorruptible and undefiled and that does not fade away, reserved in heaven for you, who are kept by the power of God through faith for salvation ready to be revealed in the last time.

—1 PETER 1:3–5

But now Christ is risen from the dead, and has become the firstfruits of those who have fallen asleep. For since by man came death, by Man also came the resurrection of the dead. For as in Adam all die, even so in Christ all shall be made alive.

—1 CORINTHIANS 15:20–22

And you, being dead in your trespasses and the uncircumcision of your flesh, He has made alive together with Him, having forgiven you all trespasses, having wiped out the handwriting of requirements that was against us, which was contrary to us. And He has taken it out of the way, having nailed it to the cross.

—COLOSSIANS 2:13–14

Offering the New Life to Others, Through My 'Walk'

"Let your light so shine before men, that they may see your good works and glorify your Father in heaven."

—MATTHEW 5:16

To the weak I became as weak, that I might win the weak. I have become all things to all men, that I might by all means save some. Now this I do for the gospel's sake, that I may be partaker of it with you. Do you not know that those who run in a race all run, but one receives the prize? Run in such a way that you may obtain it.

And everyone who competes for the prize is temperate in all things. Now they do it to obtain a perishable crown, but we for an imperishable crown. Therefore I run thus: not with uncertainty. Thus I fight: not as one who beats the air. But I discipline my body and bring it into subjection, lest, when I have preached to others, I myself should become disqualified.

—1 CORINTHIANS 9:22-27

Now thanks be to God who always leads us in triumph in Christ, and through us diffuses the fragrance of His knowledge in every place. For we are to God the fragrance of Christ among those who are being saved and among those who are perishing. To the one we are the aroma of death leading to death, and to the other the aroma of life to life. And who is sufficient for these things? For we are not, as so many, peddling the word of God; but as of sincerity, but as from God, we speak in the sight of God in Christ.

—2 CORINTHIANS 2:14-17

For this reason we also, since the day we heard it, do not cease to pray for you, and to ask that you may be filled with the knowledge of His will in all wisdom and spiritual understanding; that you may walk worthy of the Lord, fully pleasing Him, being fruitful in every good work and increasing in the knowledge of God; strengthened with all might, according to His glorious power, for all patience and longsuffering with joy; giving thanks to the Father who has qualified us to be partakers of the inheritance of the saints in the light.

—COLOSSIANS 1:9-12

Walk in the Spirit, and you shall not fulfill the lust of the flesh. For the flesh lusts against the

Spirit, and the Spirit against the flesh; and these are contrary to one another, so that you do not do the things that you wish.

—GALATIANS 5:16–17

This I say, therefore, and testify in the Lord, that you should no longer walk as the rest of the Gentiles walk, in the futility of their mind, having their understanding darkened, being alienated from the life of God, because of the ignorance that is in them, because of the hardening of their heart; who, being past feeling, have given themselves over to licentiousness, to work all uncleanness with greediness.

But you have not so learned Christ, if indeed you have heard Him and have been taught by Him, as the truth is in Jesus: that you put off, concerning your former conduct, the old man which grows corrupt according to the deceitful lusts, and be renewed in the spirit of your mind, and put on the new man which was created according to God, in righteousness and true holiness.

—EPHESIANS 4:17–24

For you were once darkness, but now you are light in the Lord. Walk as children of light (for the fruit of the Spirit is in all goodness, righteousness, and truth), proving what is acceptable to the Lord.

—EPHESIANS 5:8–10

And do this, knowing the time, that now it is high time to awake out of sleep; for now our salvation is nearer than when we first believed. The night is far spent, the day is at hand. Therefore let us cast off the works of darkness, and let us put on the armor of light. Let us walk properly, as in the day, not in revelry and drunkenness, not in licentiousness and lewdness, not in strife and envy. But put on the Lord Jesus Christ, and make no provision for the flesh, to fulfill its lusts.

—ROMANS 13:11–14

For we have spent enough of our past lifetime in doing the will of the Gentiles—when we walked in licentiousness, lusts, drunkenness, revelries, drinking parties, and abominable idolatries.

—1 PETER 4:3

Therefore, since we have this ministry, as we have received mercy, we do not lose heart. But we have renounced the hidden things of shame, not walking in craftiness nor handling the word of God deceitfully, but by manifestation of the truth commending ourselves to every man's conscience in the sight of God.

—2 CORINTHIANS 4:1–2

In all things showing yourself to be a pattern of good works; in doctrine showing integrity, reverence, incorruptibility, sound speech that cannot be condemned, that one who is an opponent may be ashamed, having nothing evil to say of you.

—TITUS 2:7–8

But sanctify the Lord God in your hearts, and always be ready to give a defense to everyone who asks you a reason for the hope that is in you, with meekness and fear; having a good conscience, that when they defame you as evildoers, those who revile your good conduct in Christ may be ashamed.

—1 PETER 3:15–16

Offering the New Life to Others, Through My Words

Now all things are of God, who has reconciled us to Himself through Jesus Christ, and has given us the ministry of reconciliation, that is, that God was in Christ reconciling the world to Himself, not imputing their trespasses to them, and has committed to us the word of reconciliation. Therefore we are ambassadors for Christ, as though God were pleading through us: we implore you on Christ's behalf, be reconciled to God.

—2 CORINTHIANS 5:18–20

Then the eleven disciples went away into Galilee, to the mountain which Jesus had appointed for them. And when they saw Him, they worshiped Him; but some doubted.

Then Jesus came and spoke to them, saying, "All authority has been given to Me in heaven and on earth. Go therefore and make disciples of all the nations, baptizing them in the name of the

Father and of the Son and of the Holy Spirit, teaching them to observe all things that I have commanded you; and lo, I am with you always, even to the end of the age." Amen.

—MATTHEW 28:16–20

John answered and said, "A man can receive nothing unless it has been given to him from heaven. You yourselves bear me witness, that I said, 'I am not the Christ,' but, 'I have been sent before Him.' He who has the bride is the bridegroom; but the friend of the bridegroom, who stands and hears him, rejoices greatly because of the bridegroom's voice. Therefore this joy of mine is fulfilled. He must increase, but I must decrease. He who comes from above is above all; he who is of the earth is earthly and speaks of the earth. He who comes from heaven is above all. And what He has seen and heard, that He testifies; and no one receives His testimony. He who has received His testimony has certified that God is true. For He whom God has sent speaks the words of God."

—JOHN 3:27–34

"But you shall receive power when the Holy Spirit has come upon you; and you shall be witnesses to Me in Jerusalem, and in all Judea and Samaria, and to the end of the earth."

—ACTS 1:8

To them God willed to make known what are the riches of the glory of this mystery among the

Gentiles: which is Christ in you, the hope of glory. Him we preach, warning every man and teaching every man in all wisdom, that we may present every man perfect in Christ Jesus. To this end I also labor, striving according to His working which works in me mightily.

—COLOSSIANS 1:27–29

■ Proclaiming with Boldness

The Example of Peter

Peter, standing up with the eleven, raised his voice and said to them, "Men of Judea and all who dwell in Jerusalem, let this be known to you, and heed my words. For these are not drunk, as you suppose, since it is only the third hour of the day. But this is what was spoken by the prophet Joel:

'And it shall come to pass in the last days,
  says God,
That I will pour out of My Spirit on all flesh;
Your sons and your daughters shall prophesy,
Your young men shall see visions,
Your old men shall dream dreams.
And on My menservants and on My
  maidservants
I will pour out My Spirit in those days;
And they shall prophesy.
I will show wonders in heaven above
And signs in the earth beneath:
Blood and fire and vapor of smoke.

The sun shall be turned into darkness,
And the moon into blood,
Before the coming of the great and notable day
of the LORD.
And it shall come to pass that whoever calls
on the name of the LORD shall be saved.'

"Men of Israel, hear these words: Jesus of Nazareth, a Man attested by God to you by miracles, wonders, and signs which God did through Him in your midst, as you yourselves also know—Him, being delivered by the determined purpose and foreknowledge of God, you have taken by lawless hands, have crucified, and put to death; whom God raised up, having loosed the pains of death, because it was not possible that He should be held by it. For David says concerning Him:

'I foresaw the LORD always before my face,
For He is at my right hand, that I may not be
shaken.
Therefore my heart rejoiced, and my tongue
was glad;
Moreover my flesh also will rest in hope.
Because You will not leave my soul in Hades,
Nor will You allow Your Holy One to see
corruption.
You have made known to me the ways of life;
You will make me full of joy in Your presence.'

"Men and brethren, let me speak freely to you of the patriarch David, that he is both dead and buried, and his tomb is with us to this day. Therefore, being a prophet, and knowing that God had sworn with an oath to him that of the fruit of his body, according to the flesh, He would raise up the Christ to sit on his throne, he, foreseeing this, spoke concerning the resurrection of the Christ, that His soul was not left in Hades, nor did His flesh see corruption. This Jesus God has raised up, of which we are all witnesses."

—ACTS 2:14–32

The Example of Paul

Then Paul stood up, and motioning with his hand said, "Men of Israel, and you who fear God, listen: The God of this people Israel chose our fathers, and exalted the people when they dwelt as strangers in the land of Egypt, and with an up-lifted arm He brought them out of it. Now for a time of about forty years He put up with their ways in the wilderness. And when He had destroyed seven nations in the land of Canaan, He distributed their land to them by allotment. After that He gave them judges for about four hundred and fifty years, until Samuel the prophet. And afterward they asked for a king; so God gave them Saul the son of Kish, a man of the tribe of Benjamin, for forty years. And when He had removed him, He raised up for them David as king, to whom also He gave testimony and said,

'I have found David the son of Jesse, a man after My own heart, who will do all My will.'

"From this man's seed, according to the promise, God raised up for Israel a Savior—Jesus—after John had first preached, before His coming, the baptism of repentance to all the people of Israel. And as John was finishing his course, he said, 'Who do you think I am? I am not He. But behold, there comes One after me, the sandals of whose feet I am not worthy to loose.'

"Men and brethren, sons of the family of Abraham, and those among you who fear God, to you the word of this salvation has been sent. For those who dwell in Jerusalem, and their rulers, because they did not know Him, nor even the voices of the Prophets which are read every Sabbath, have fulfilled them in condemning Him. And though they found no cause for death in Him, they asked Pilate that He should be put to death. Now when they had fulfilled all that was written concerning Him, they took Him down from the tree and laid Him in a tomb. But God raised Him from the dead.

"He was seen for many days by those who came up with Him from Galilee to Jerusalem, who are His witnesses to the people. And we declare to you glad tidings."

—ACTS 13:16–32

■ Encouraging with Gentleness

Brethren, if a man is overtaken in any trespass, you who are spiritual restore such a one in a spirit of gentleness, considering yourself lest you also be tempted. Bear one another's burdens, and so fulfill the law of Christ.

—GALATIANS 6:1–2

Now we exhort you, brethren, warn those who are unruly, comfort the fainthearted, uphold the weak, be patient with all.

—1 THESSALONIANS 5:14

Brethren, if anyone among you wanders from the truth, and someone turns him back, let him know that he who turns a sinner from the error of his way will save a soul from death and cover a multitude of sins.

—JAMES 5:19–20

Living the Life of Praise

The previous chapter stressed maintaining your new lifestyle by carrying the recovery message to others. Part of that maintenance program involves regular meditation on the Scriptures. That's because a focus on self needs to be balanced with a focus on the creator and preserver of self—God.

Surprisingly, losing ourselves in worship and praise "pays off" in significant inner joy. So here's a chapter just for the joy of it! What better place to go than to the psalms for the epitome of the human heart's expression of adoration for the Almighty?

Praise for the Greatness of Creation

O Lord, our Lord,
How excellent is Your name in all the earth,
You who set Your glory above the heavens!
Out of the mouth of babes and infants

You have ordained strength,
Because of Your enemies,
That You may silence the enemy and the
    avenger.
When I consider Your heavens, the work of
    Your fingers,
The moon and the stars, which You have
    ordained,
What is man that You are mindful of him,
And the son of man that You visit him?
For You have made him a little lower than the
    angels,
And You have crowned him with glory and
    honor.
You have made him to have dominion over the
    works of Your hands;
You have put all things under his feet,
All sheep and oxen—
Even the beasts of the field,
The birds of the air,
And the fish of the sea
That pass through the paths of the seas.
O LORD, our Lord,
How excellent is Your name in all the earth!
                                    —PSALM 8:1–9

The earth is the LORD's, and all its fullness,
The world and those who dwell therein.
For He has founded it upon the seas,
And established it upon the waters.
Who may ascend into the hill of the LORD?
Or who may stand in His holy place? . . .

Lift up your heads, O you gates!
And be lifted up, you everlasting doors!
And the King of glory shall come in.
Who is this King of glory?
The LORD strong and mighty,
The LORD mighty in battle.
Lift up your heads, O you gates!
And be lifted up, you everlasting doors!
And the King of glory shall come in.
Who is this King of glory?
The LORD of hosts,
He is the King of glory.

—PSALM 24:1–10

Praise for the LORD's Voice

Give unto the LORD, O you mighty ones,
Give unto the LORD glory and strength.
Give unto the LORD the glory due to His
   name;
Worship the LORD in the beauty of holiness.
The voice of the LORD is over the waters;
The God of glory thunders;
The LORD is over many waters.
The voice of the LORD is powerful;
The voice of the LORD is full of majesty.
The voice of the LORD breaks the cedars,
Yes, the LORD splinters the cedars of Lebanon.
He makes them also skip like a calf,
Lebanon and Sirion like a young wild ox.

The voice of the LORD divides the flames of
    fire.
The voice of the LORD shakes the wilderness;
The LORD shakes the Wilderness of Kadesh.
The voice of the LORD makes the deer give
    birth,
And strips the forests bare;
And in His temple everyone says, "Glory!"
—PSALM 29:1–9

Praise for Deliverance from Trouble and Enemies

I will bless the LORD at all times;
His praise shall continually be in my mouth.
My soul shall make its boast in the LORD;
The humble shall hear of it and be glad.
Oh, magnify the LORD with me,
And let us exalt His name together.
I sought the LORD, and He heard me,
And delivered me from all my fears.
They looked to Him and were radiant,
And their faces were not ashamed.
This poor man cried out, and the LORD heard
    him,
And saved him out of all his troubles.
The angel of the LORD encamps all around
    those who fear Him,
And delivers them.
Oh, taste and see that the LORD is good;

Blessed is the man who trusts in Him!
—PSALM 34:1–8

I will praise You, O Lord, with my whole
 heart;
I will tell of all Your marvelous works.
I will be glad and rejoice in You;
I will sing praise to Your name, O Most High.
When my enemies turn back,
They shall fall and perish at Your presence.
For You have maintained my right and my
 cause;
You sat on the throne judging in
 righteousness.
You have rebuked the nations,
You have destroyed the wicked;
You have blotted out their name forever and
 ever.
—PSALM 9:1–5

Come, behold the works of the Lord,
Who has made desolations in the earth.
He makes wars cease to the end of the earth;
He breaks the bow and cuts the spear in two;
He burns the chariot in the fire.
Be still, and know that I am God;
I will be exalted among the nations,
I will be exalted in the earth!
The Lord of hosts is with us;
The God of Jacob is our refuge.
—PSALM 46:8–11

Oh, clap your hands, all you peoples!
Shout to God with the voice of triumph!
For the LORD Most High is awesome;
He is a great King over all the earth.
He will subdue the peoples under us,
And the nations under our feet.
He will choose our inheritance for us,
The excellence of Jacob whom He loves. Selah
God has gone up with a shout,
The LORD with the sound of a trumpet.
Sing praises to God, sing praises!
Sing praises to our King, sing praises!
For God is the King of all the earth;
Sing praises with understanding.
God reigns over the nations;
God sits on His holy throne.
The princes of the people have gathered
    together,
The people of the God of Abraham.
For the shields of the earth belong to God;
He is greatly exalted.

—PSALM 47:1-9

Praise for God's Rule over Nature

By awesome deeds in righteousness You will
    answer us,
O God of our salvation,
You who are the confidence of all the ends of
    the earth,

And of the far-off seas;
Who established the mountains by His
    strength,
Being clothed with power;
You who still the noise of the seas,
The noise of their waves,
And the tumult of the peoples.
They also who dwell in the farthest parts are
    afraid of Your signs;
You make the outgoings of the morning and
    evening rejoice.
You visit the earth and water it,
You greatly enrich it;
The river of God is full of water;
You provide their grain,
For so You have prepared it.
You water its ridges abundantly,
You settle its furrows;
You make it soft with showers,
You bless its growth.
You crown the year with Your goodness,
And Your paths drip with abundance.
They drop on the pastures of the wilderness,
And the little hills rejoice on every side.
The pastures are clothed with flocks;
The valleys also are covered with grain;
They shout for joy, they also sing.

—PSALM 65:5–13

The LORD reigns, He is clothed with majesty;
The LORD is clothed,
He has girded Himself with strength.

Surely the world is established, so that it
    cannot be moved.
Your throne is established from of old;
You are from everlasting.
The floods have lifted up, O LORD,
The floods have lifted up their voice;
The floods lift up their waves.
The LORD on high is mightier
Than the noise of many waters,
Than the mighty waves of the sea.
Your testimonies are very sure;
Holiness adorns Your house,
O LORD, forever.

—PSALM 93:1–5

May the glory of the LORD endure forever;
May the LORD rejoice in His works.
He looks on the earth, and it trembles;
He touches the hills, and they smoke.
I will sing to the LORD as long as I live;
I will sing praise to my God while I have my
    being.

—PSALM 104:31–33

Praise for God's Reality over Idols

Why should the Gentiles say,
"Where now is their God?"
But our God is in heaven;
He does whatever He pleases.
Their idols are silver and gold,

The work of men's hands.
They have mouths, but they do not speak;
Eyes they have, but they do not see;
They have ears, but they do not hear;
Noses they have, but they do not smell;
They have hands, but they do not handle;
Feet they have, but they do not walk;
Nor do they mutter through their throat.
Those who make them are like them;
So is everyone who trusts in them. . . .
You who fear the LORD, trust in the LORD;
He is their help and their shield. . . .
The heaven, even the heavens, are the LORD's;
But the earth He has given to the children of
    men.
The dead do not praise the LORD,
Nor any who go down into silence.
But we will bless the LORD
From this time forth and forevermore.
Praise the LORD!

—PSALM 115:2–8, 11, 16–18

Praise for God's Knowledge of My Inner Being

O LORD, You have searched me and known
    me.
You know my sitting down and my rising up;
You understand my thought afar off.
You comprehend my path and my lying
    down,
And are acquainted with all my ways. . . .

How precious also are Your thoughts to me, O
   God!
How great is the sum of them!
If I should count them, they would be more in
   number than the sand;
When I awake, I am still with You.

—PSALM 139:1–3, 17–18

Praise the LORD! Praise the LORD, O my soul!
While I live I will praise the LORD;
I will sing praises to my God while I have my
   being.
Do not put your trust in princes,
Nor in a son of man, in whom there is no
   help.
His spirit departs, he returns to his earth;
In that very day his plans perish.
Happy is he who has the God of Jacob for his
   help,
Whose hope is in the LORD his God.

—PSALM 146:1–5

Praise for God's Providential Care

Praise the LORD!
For it is good to sing praises to our God;
For it is pleasant, and praise is beautiful.
The LORD builds up Jerusalem;
He gathers together the outcasts of Israel.
He heals the broken-hearted
And binds up their wounds.

He counts the number of the stars;
He calls them all by name.
Great is our Lord, and mighty in power;
His understanding is infinite.
The LORD lifts up the humble;
He casts the wicked down to the ground.
Sing to the LORD with thanksgiving;
Sing praises on the harp to our God,
Who covers the heavens with clouds,
Who prepares rain for the earth,
Who makes grass to grow on the mountains.
He gives to the beast its food,
And to the young ravens that cry.
He does not delight in the strength of the
   horse;
He takes no pleasure in the legs of a man.
The LORD takes pleasure in those who fear
   Him,
In those who hope in His mercy.
                              —PSALM 147:1-11

[He] made heaven and earth,
The sea, and all that is in them;
Who keeps truth forever,
Who executes justice for the oppressed,
Who gives food to the hungry.
The LORD gives freedom to the prisoners.
The LORD opens the eyes of the blind;
The LORD raises those who are bowed down;
The LORD loves the righteous.
The LORD watches over the strangers;

He relieves the fatherless and widow;
But the way of the wicked He turns upside
   down.
The LORD shall reign forever—
Your God, O Zion, to all generations.
Praise the LORD!

—PSALM 146:6–10

Praise, Morning and Night

O God, You are my God;
Early will I seek You;
My soul thirsts for You;
My flesh longs for You
In a dry and thirsty land
Where there is no water.

—PSALM 63:1

Awake, lute and harp!
I will awaken the dawn.
I will praise You, O LORD, among the peoples,
And I will sing praises to You among the
   nations.
For Your mercy is great above the heavens,
And Your truth reaches to the clouds.
Be exalted, O God, above the heavens,
And Your glory above all the earth;
That Your beloved may be delivered,
Save with Your right hand, and hear me.

—PSALM 108:2–6

From the rising of the sun to its going down
The LORD's name is to be praised.

—PSALM 113:3

Behold, bless the LORD,
All you servants of the LORD,
Who by night stand in the house of the LORD!
Lift up your hands in the sanctuary,
And bless the LORD.

—PSALM 134:1-3

Praise in the Sanctuary

So I have looked for You in the sanctuary,
To see Your power and Your glory.
Because Your lovingkindness is better than
   life,
My lips shall praise You.
Thus I will bless You while I live;
I will lift up my hands in Your name.
My soul shall be satisfied as with marrow and
   fatness,
And my mouth shall praise You with joyful
   lips.

—PSALM 63:2-5

I will go into Your house with burnt offerings;
I will pay You my vows,
Which my lips have uttered
And my mouth has spoken when I was in
   trouble.

I will offer You burnt sacrifices of fat animals,
With the sweet aroma of rams;
I will offer bulls with goats.
Come and hear, all you who fear God,
And I will declare what He has done for my
    soul.
I cried to Him with my mouth,
And He was extolled with my tongue.
If I regard iniquity in my heart,
The LORD will not hear.
But certainly God has heard me;
He has attended to the voice of my prayer.
Blessed be God,
Who has not turned away my prayer,
Nor His mercy from me!

—PSALM 66:13–20

Praise the LORD!
Praise God in His sanctuary;
Praise Him in His mighty firmament!
Praise Him for His mighty acts;
Praise Him according to His excellent
    greatness!

—PSALM 150:1–2

Praise with Singing and Shouting

Oh come, let us sing to the LORD!
Let us shout joyfully to the Rock of our
    salvation.

Let us come before His presence with
     thanksgiving;
Let us shout joyfully to Him with psalms.
For the LORD is the great God,
And the great King above all gods.
In His hand are the deep places of the earth;
The heights of the hills are His also.
The sea is His, for He made it;
And His hands formed the dry land.
Oh come, let us worship and bow down;
Let us kneel before the LORD our Maker.
For He is our God,
And we are the people of His pasture,
And the sheep of His hand.

—PSALM 95:1-7

Oh, sing to the LORD a new song!
For He has done marvelous things;
His right hand and His holy arm have gained
     Him the victory.
The LORD has made known His salvation;
His righteousness He has openly shown in the
     sight of the nations.
He has remembered His mercy and His
     faithfulness to the house of Israel;
All the ends of the earth have seen the
     salvation of our God.
Shout joyfully to the LORD, all the earth;
Break forth in song, rejoice, and sing praises.
Sing to the LORD with the harp,
With the harp and the sound of a psalm,
With trumpets and the sound of a horn;

Shout joyfully before the LORD, the King.
—PSALM 98:1-6

Make a joyful shout to the LORD, all you
    lands!
Serve the LORD with gladness;
Come before His presence with singing.
Know that the LORD, He is God;
It is He who has made us, and not we
    ourselves;
We are His people and the sheep of His
    pasture.
Enter into His gates with thanksgiving,
And into His courts with praise.
Be thankful to Him, and bless His name.
For the LORD is good;
His mercy is everlasting,
And His truth endures to all generations.
—PSALM 100:1-5

Praise with Musical Instruments

Rejoice in the LORD, O you righteous!
For praise from the upright is beautiful.
Praise the LORD with the harp;
Make melody to Him with an instrument of
    ten strings.
Sing to Him a new song;
Play skillfully with a shout of joy.
For the word of the LORD is right,
And all His work is done in truth.

He loves righteousness and justice;
The earth is full of the goodness of the LORD.
—PSALM 33:1–5

Praise Him with the sound of the trumpet;
Praise Him with the lute and harp!
Praise Him with the timbrel and dance;
Praise Him with stringed instruments and
    flutes!
Praise Him with loud cymbals;
Praise Him with high sounding cymbals!
Let everything that has breath praise the
    LORD.
Praise the LORD!
—PSALM 150:3–6

Praise, Praise, Praise: from Every Created Thing

Praise Him, all His angels;
Praise Him, all His hosts!
Praise Him, sun and moon;
Praise Him, all you stars of light!
Praise Him, you heavens of heavens,
And you waters above the heavens!
Let them praise the name of the LORD,
For He commanded and they were created.
He has also established them forever and ever;
He has made a decree which shall not pass
    away.
Praise the LORD from the earth,

You great sea creatures and all the depths;
Fire and hail, snow and clouds;
Stormy wind, fulfilling His word;
Mountains and all hills;
Fruitful trees and all cedars;
Beasts and all cattle;
Creeping things and flying fowl;
Kings of the earth and all peoples;
Princes and all judges of the earth;
Both young men and maidens;
Old men and children.
Let them praise the name of the LORD,
For His name alone is exalted;
His glory is above the earth and heaven.
And He has exalted the horn of His people,
The praise of all His saints—
Of the children of Israel,
A people near to Him.
Praise the LORD!

—PSALM 148:2–14

Index

Old Testament

New Testament